With Trust in Place

Writing from the Outside

About the Author

Alice Leahy is Director of Trust, a non-judgemental, befriending social and health service for people who are homeless, which she co-founded in the mid-1970s. She is also a writer, commentator, broadcaster and lecturer promoting understanding of the needs of the outsider in our society. Her first book, *Not Just a Bed for the Night*, was co-authored with Anne Dempsey (1995).

Her work has been recognised with several awards over the years, including a Person of the Year Award (1988); Carers Award (1992); Lord Mayor's Award (1993) and an Honorary Fellowship from the Faculty of Nursing and Midwifery, Royal College of Surgeons in Ireland (1999). Alice sees these awards as recognition of the work of Trust.

With Trust in Place

Writing from the Outside

Edited by Alice Leahy

TOWN
HOUSE
DUBLIN

First published in 2003 by

TownHouse, Dublin
THCH Ltd
Trinity House
Charleston Road
Ranelagh
Dublin 6
Ireland

A CIP catalogue record for this book is available from
the British Library.

ISBN: 1-86059-189-2

Cover design by Anú Design, Tara
Printed by Rotanor, Norway 2003

CONTENTS

ACKNOWLEDGMENTS

Trust's work and survival over the years is due to the enormous support, both moral and financial, received from people in all walks of life, without which we could not continue to help the people we meet everyday.

This book was made possible by extraordinary and unstinting co-operation from a large and diverse cross-section of people, family and friends simply too numerous to mention.

To everyone who has contributed to this book and our publisher – we are extremely grateful and very much appreciate their encouragement, which more than anything helps to keep us going.

Some of the contributors have given names to the people they have written about. These names are not the real names of the people involved, but are pseudonyms to protect their anonymity.

Alice Leahy
August 2003

INTRODUCTION

When I mentioned this book on the theme of 'The Outsider' to Kevin, one of the men who is homeless who comes into us regularly, and asked him to suggest a title, he said, 'Outsiders have the head well screwed on but go against the tread!'

We work with people like Kevin who, because they 'go against the tread', find themselves on the margins of society and find their way to our door every day in increasing numbers.

We are a small agency. We provide a daily place of refuge for those who feel excluded by society. We do not ask them to fill in forms. We do not ask questions. If people choose to talk, we listen. We provide what medical help we can. A change of clothes. A shower. Anything we can to make a life on the outside a little more bearable.

This book grew out of our increasing frustration that our approach is regarded as almost subversive because we refuse to delve in an invasive way into the private lives of society's most vulnerable, many of whom are on the outside precisely because they cannot cope with that level of scrutiny.

Very little has changed since the mid-1970s when we first went out to 'skippers' – derelict buildings, old tree trunks, abandoned cars, anywhere people found shelter – to provide what help we could. Today this is called a multi-disciplinary approach except, unlike us, most professionals and managers supervise the process from their desks and do not go out and meet people on the ground. The managers of the 'services' have become more and more remote from the people they serve.

This modern approach requires agencies like ours to

adopt 'performance indicators' and seek to make people who are homeless conform to 'benchmarks'. In short, to subject them to a level of 'management' that drove many of them out onto the street in the first place. In other words, management means forcing people to change, which many of them are simply not able to do.

The point we are trying to make in this book is that the 'outsider' who drops in to us every day has a lot in common with the many successful outsiders celebrated in this book. They share, in a sense, the same fundamental values – they are different and maybe they even need to be different to survive.

In accommodating the outsider, we need to think in terms of accommodating diversity and creating a society that can celebrate and appreciate what makes people different. This is about creating a world where no one feels excluded and where those who are different are warmly welcomed. A world where highly talented outsiders would prosper and the others would not end up on the side of the road.

An idealistic vision?

No. We only have to look into someone's eyes and smile, especially those we usually hurry past. To raise our voice in protest against a racist remark or a social slur. To refuse to look the other way when someone is bullied. In short, we may have to make an effort to insist on making everyone feel welcome.

While in no way radical, this approach would become almost revolutionary in its impact if it could be extended in practical ways into the bureaucracy geared to tackling social exclusion, given the way the services are currently organised – something that is only obvious to those of us at the coalface.

We, like so many people in other agencies, both voluntary and statutory, are frustrated by the fact that, despite years of unparalleled prosperity, nothing seems to have changed. This led us to try to share the insights and experience we have gained through our hands-on work. The fundamental problem we seek to confront is that those managing the system appear to have lost touch with what is happening on the ground. The more resources they deploy, the less impact they have because those who should be consulted are not asked for their opinions. Those, like us, who put the personal and human needs of people who are on the margins first are deemed not to be using 'best practice', are not progressive and are, therefore, dismissed.

Despite our small size, we felt that unless we tried to bring the reality of life for the outsiders we meet every day to the attention of the wider community, nothing would ever change. We were also acutely aware that many others working with the disadvantaged and the marginalised also see the urgency of doing this but many are not in a position to speak out for fear of losing their job or their agency having their funding cut.

Putting our philosophy into action is a constant and persistent challenge. This was brought home to me forcefully one day by a retired man I met at a social function. He asked, 'What do you call them?', referring to the people we work with.

'People,' I replied. But he persisted, 'You must call them something?' We parted company.

One reason we have been able to undertake a level of work in this area, which is normally only deemed possible by the largest of organisations, is through our adoption of the internet as a vehicle for that awareness raising. In that regard, our website – www.trust-ireland.ie – has been vital.

Our efforts to share our experience and insights began initially with an education programme and a national essay competition in 2000–2001, this was followed in 2002–2003 with a national art competition. Both of these generated a very perceptive and encouraging response from students all over Ireland.

This book grew out of our commitment to education and, through co-operation from a very diverse, experienced and distinguished group of contributors, we hope to take that debate further by enabling anyone who picks up this book to experience some sense of what it means to be an outsider and what it is possible to achieve.

Non-judgemental is a word that is often used to describe our approach and, maybe more than anything, it is why the people we meet every day find Trust a safe place and why people continue to want to help us to do the work we do.

Our work would not be possible without support from all sections of the community. The people who enable us to give out almost 400 outfits a month, all good as new and given freely as part of our holistic health service and primary care commitment. The man who delivers three boxes of fruit a week, the much-improved skin conditions proof of its value. The financial and material help we get from the Health Board. The support of Dublin City Council and our premises from the Iveagh Trust. We acknowledge those who send us money, cards and letters. The woman who sends us photos of her pets reminds us that we share our world with other creatures and that those who visit us with their pets are not refused help.

If we are to create a world where diversity is accommodated, it must be a place where those who are different are allowed the freedom to be themselves.

This book is a celebration of outsiders, and is part of our effort to help create a suitable environment for change by sharing the experience we have gained in working over the years with people seen as not being successful in society's eyes.

We at Trust intend to remain outsiders, because we see it as a position of strength and not of weakness.

The contributors to this book show that people who go against the tread enrich us all: from Kevin who gave me the opening paragraph for this introduction, to the giants of Irish society, like the late Noël Browne, who features in this book and who I remember with fondness sitting in the middle of a small city-centre complex with people about to be evicted so many years ago.

The title of this book was taken from Bernard Farrell's contribution which looks at a prison experience and the strength of the human spirit which could have been destroyed were it not for the vision of an outsider. This same vision was very much responsible for the setting up of Trust.

The philosophy of Trust is based on two central principles. The recognition of every individual's right to be treated as an autonomous and unique human being and the need to restore the dignity of individuals who society has labelled deviant and undesirable.

Daily we meet people whose bodies are ravaged by disease and violence, who may have pressure sores from sleeping out in all weathers, because they may have been sleeping in urine-soaked clothes for weeks. They can have infected and untreated minor skin conditions and major skin problems, like leg ulcers. They may suffer from medical conditions common to the general public but exacerbated by their living conditions, such as lice-infected heads, scabies or malnutrition.

We regularly come into contact with men and women who have been abused mentally and physically, some may even be working in prostitution. We see people who have been institutionalised in psychiatric hospitals and prisons many for years who are now relocated from one institution to another (hostels) in the name of progress with insufficient support services to meet their needs. Some of these people have even found themselves to be inappropriately labelled 'mentally ill'.

These people, our friends, often struggle with guilt because they have left loved ones behind. Partners who have suffered for so long, children who are in care, parents who have died to whom they were unable to say goodbye. Drugs often dull the pain of living. Alcohol, gambling, and illegal and prescribed drugs all play a part. Many people we meet have attempted suicide and some sadly have succeeded. Some people we meet, in spite of unthinkable pain and misery, never complain, never ask for anything, accept their lot, leave us feeling challenged and inspired.

We live in a market-driven society that only sees loud and impressive actions. The little things done are usually seen as being irrelevant. Services are also driven by market forces. In Trust every morning, we meet men and women who come simply for a wash or change of clothes to make themselves feel that they are part of society and have a sense of worth. The interaction can have far more impressive outcomes than many realise and proves that success cannot be measured in the language of consumerism.

I increasingly think you have to be an outsider to work with outsiders. Anyone who takes a stand risks being excluded. The first time I realised this was as a student nurse. My fellow students and I arranged to meet Matron to complain about the patients' food. While knocking on the little brass monkey on her door, fearful of the reception we would receive, I turned around to find my colleagues retreating. I happened to be the one nearest the door. This very early experience was a sharp reminder that you risk being excluded when you rock the boat and many who attempt to make a difference become outsiders.

It may seem like a cliché to say 'there go I but for the grace of God', but thinking of the many people, including those who had no opportunities and those like former solicitors, nurses, doctors, professors, journalists, religious and even a well-known rugby player – all of whom have sought momentary refuge in Trust – one cannot help feeling it could happen to any of us.

In celebrating outsiders in this book, we are acknowledging that those who dare to be different can enrich and challenge us in very practical ways and that those who 'go against the tread' and end up on the side of the road are as worthy of our respect as those who achieve success by taking the same road.

Alice Leahy
August 2003

Dedicated to people gone before who inspire us to look at how we live in today's world and those who daily continue to challenge us.

TRUST

MAEVE BINCHY

When I knew Oliver first, he used to hum to himself in a high falsetto as he went along the road.

He would be coming from his school, with a stick that he'd rub along the railings, I from mine, with a bow on top of my head and my shiny school bag on my back. I never saw Oliver with any books or bag.

He was odd looking, I remember, in that his pullover was much too small and his shoes seemed enormous. It was as if he had left the house in his little brother's jumper and his father's shoes.

He was never with other fellows – he was always on his own.

When I was alone, we just nodded at each other. When I was with my mother, she greeted him as she greeted everyone on every street, 'How are you Oliver?' she would ask unfailingly as if one day there would be an answer.

He would hum louder by way of response.

'He's his own man, Oliver,' she would nod approvingly.

I couldn't see why she said this.

Oliver was doing all the things she didn't like done by her own flock – like running sticks along railings, like singing in the street, like not responding to grown-ups.

But then who knew what people liked?

As I got older and went to a different school, I still saw Oliver from time to time. Standing outside the cinema on his own, on a Saturday afternoon – humming away, hands in pockets, refusing any conversation.

He had a deal, apparently, which meant that he could get in free if he went around and scooped up all the cigarette butts and sweet papers afterwards.

He used to go to a bookshop too and a friend of mine who worked there part time told me that they watched him like a hawk. He looked so odd, they were sure he would nick the books but, no, he used to stand there for hours reading them, putting in a bus ticket as a bookmark to show where he had got to.

He still hummed to himself tunelessly in a lower register now, he never wanted any conversation.

I assumed that he had left school but didn't think about him much and I was very surprised when my mother said she had met him and that he had said he was going to be married.

He was about two years older than me, which would have made him nineteen. I don't know which was the more shocking about what she said: the fact that anyone would marry Oliver and listen to him humming all day, and maybe all night, or the fact that he had actually unbent enough to have a conversation with anyone.

'Who is he marrying?' I asked.

'The most beautiful girl in the world and they're saving together for a house,' my mother said, but there was something grim about her smile.

'I told Oliver they should save in a bank or a building society,' she said. 'But you know him, he just started to hum and sing again.'

'And where *are* they saving?' I wondered.

In a biscuit tin, apparently.

Oliver's beautiful girlfriend had a tin with a four-leaved clover on it and that's where his wages went every Friday. Oliver worked as a handyman or doing odd jobs on building sites, but this was the 1950s and there was little casual employment to be found in Dublin.

One Saturday night, I saw Oliver standing slightly apart from a crowd waiting to get the mail boat to England. I remember the night very well because we were there as some kind of moral support for a friend who was going to London to have her baby and then to have it adopted. A fiction had been arranged that she had a great job in market research.

That's the way things were done in those days.

They took forever to let people on to the boat and our goodbyes were endless. So I went over to talk to Oliver. He just hummed back at me until I said I heard he was marrying a beautiful girl. Then he stopped humming and told me about her.

She had golden – not fair, but golden – hair, she had eyes like big violets, they were saving for a house.

'How much have you saved already?' I asked.

Oliver had put in £317 but it should build much faster once he got a job in London. He would be able to send at least £12 every Friday.

He still looked awkwardly dressed, he wore a funny knitted hat and he had a habit of looking not at you but beyond you, as if the real person he was talking to were standing right behind you.

You know, I envied Oliver at that moment, he was so sure and happy, so delighted with his golden-haired and violet-eyed princess, so willing to go and work hard for her and her biscuit tin of savings.

We were a very confused group, with our friend going to give away the child of the man she loved because he had forgotten to tell her that he was engaged to someone else.

Our own futures seemed bewildering and anxious too. How did you know what love was if this catastrophe could happen to one of our nearest friends? In comparison, Oliver seemed a rock of strength and confidence.

I remember the peach-coloured sunset and the mail boat hooting as it pulled out of Dún Laoghaire harbour with its hundreds of life stories on board.

It's all as clear in my mind as if it were yesterday.

It's the years after that things get a bit blurry.

Our friend in London had her baby girl, gave up her daughter for adoption and came back with hard, cold eyes.

She eventually married a man she barely knew. None of us were invited to her wedding because we knew her past. She had two sons and, when the younger one was five, she died from an accidental overdose of sleeping pills, which had never been prescribed, washed down by vodka, a drink she never normally touched.

As we stood at her Funeral Mass, I wondered about Oliver and hoped that his trip to England that night ten long years before had been a luckier one. I must ask my mother, I thought, did he come home and marry his princess? Did she really have violet eyes?

'Saddest thing that ever happened,' my mother said.

He sent money month after month and, when she had enough, she upped and went off. She left him a note: 'Sorry Oliver things just got too much for me.' Oliver's mother found the note on her mat and went to find the golden princess but it was too late.

So Oliver's mother went to the boarding house where he stayed in London and told him.

In the boarding house, they told him that Oliver had sent her almost every penny he earned, he had bought no clothes, he never had a packet of cigarettes or a pint.

While she sat there and told him that the princess and the biscuit tin had gone forever from his life, he started humming again, tunelessly, to himself.

He wouldn't discuss it. If things had got too much for her then that's what had happened, perhaps he shouldn't have stayed away from her for so long, she was lonely waiting for him and it had upset her mind.

To say anything against the girl who had disappeared with his life savings only drove him into frenzy. So his mother brought him home back to Ireland and, because he was practically in rags, she asked around until she got him a few clothes to wear.

For years I used to see him in a tweed jacket that had once belonged to my father and, in cold weather, he had wrapped around his neck several times a school scarf from Blackrock College that someone else must have donated. He wore a black cowboy hat as well and seemed well equipped for his job as the person who opened and closed the gates in a big business, and who also had responsibility for sweeping its yard and tearing up cardboard boxes.

As it happened, I used to pass the place he worked when I was on my own way to work and we would greet each other from time to time.

Some days it would be a bit of humming but others he would ask questions that were sharper and more relevant than anyone else's.

'Is there anything wrong in your family?' he asked.

There was – my mother was dying. I asked him how he knew. He said he could see it on our faces.

'Tell her I don't think it will be too bad,' he said. 'Promise?'

I said I would but I didn't because those were the days when we didn't admit that people were dying, we pretended to them that they were getting better.

'Did you give her my message?' he asked me.

Things were so bad then I had no problem in lying to him.

'And what did she say?' I had forgotten how very persistent Oliver could be.

He didn't look at me, he looked over my shoulder as always waiting for the reply.

So what could I say? Suddenly, I remembered something my mother *had* said about Oliver years back when the world was young.

'She said, "Oliver is his own man."'

He thought about it and nodded, satisfied.

'Yes that's what she'd say all right,' he agreed.

It was as if he had tested it and found that it had an authenticity for him.

When she died, he was there at the church still wearing my father's old tweed jacket and humming to himself.

In the memories of that day, I can see him clearly, his cowboy hat held to his chest and his head lowered in respect as the mourning car drove by.

Things changed then for everyone.

The big business firm where Oliver worked was sold and became a clutch of town houses and they didn't need Oliver to open gates or sweep yards any more.

And I didn't have that sure touch that my mother had of offering people clothes without offending them.

The Blackrock College scarf had grown thin and my father's tweed jacket had fallen off him. But he was still tall and smiling and humming to himself as he walked from one end of the street showing equal interest in borrowing and lending rates at a building society, bags of potatoes, ladies' shoes or power drills. Whatever was on display, he window-shopped.

His mother said that he was the best son she could have been given. He painted the place inside and out for her, he did the shopping, he neither drank nor smoked, he had found her the cheapest television in the borough.

'Wasn't it a pity that that girl he had disappeared on him that time?' I said going into forbidden territory.

'That girl was always going to disappear,' Oliver's mother said. 'Much better earlier than later. She was a drug addict. She's dead now, Lord have mercy on her.'

Oliver's mother didn't expect or want the Lord to have *much* mercy on her you felt.

'Does Oliver know?'

'Do you know I have no idea. Every time I tried to tell him, he just sang louder and louder, it's a way he has of dealing with the world, all that humming and singing.'

Oliver's mother is ninety now, she likes to be in her own home with her own son.

At first, and entirely for her own good, social welfare wondered if Oliver would be a fit person to look after her. He came and asked me to speak for him.

I told them that he was his own man and that humming was his way of dealing with the world and somehow, wonderfully and magically, they all agreed.

Maeve Binchy

THE PEOPLE'S SOLICITOR

GERARD BRADY

The law is not generally considered to be a caring profession, in the sense that medicine, for example, is. Yet, there have always been lawyers who saw their service to the community as more than just a means of securing their livelihood or perhaps even enriching themselves. Such a one was Caoimghin MacCathmhaoil who, in more than half a century's practice as a solicitor, acquired the reputation of being always more concerned with serving others than with any gain that might accrue to him in the process.

Caoimghin was born in Swinford, County Mayo, in March 1920, third of the six children of Tomás Mac-Cathmhaoil and Bríd Bradley. His father, a solicitor since 1914, was deeply involved in the Anglo-Irish War of Independence as a guerrilla fighter and was later a judge of the courts system established under the First Dáil Éireann. The war climaxed in 1920, which was to be remembered as 'The Year of the Terror', when Lloyd George, frustrated by the failure of conventional military measures, unleashed the brutality of the so-called Black and Tans and the Auxiliaries upon city and country. Tomás MacCathmhaoil was imprisoned that year and again during the Civil War, when he was among those who opposed the Treaty settlement. These were bleak times for his wife Bríd and their children, but brighter times beckoned in 1932 when, on his appointment as County Registrar, they moved to Wicklow and that, thereafter, became the family home.

Caoimghin pursued his secondary studies with the Cistercians at Mount Melleray, after which he was articled to his father and took the Law Society course before being enrolled as a solicitor in 1944 when he returned to Swinford to practise in his father's former office.

Caoimghin was a happy young man, quite handsome, a keen fisherman and athletic, though he never achieved championship status. With some friends, he owned a small boat called *An Faoláin*, from which they regularly fished along the east coast. He was a good runner, too, and, years later even in his seventies, he was proud of his ability to sprint across Eyre Square in Galway to catch the Dublin train just as it was about to depart. Cycling was another pastime and, with his brothers Pádraic and Sean, he cycled more than once across the country to their old home in Swinford.

From his earliest years, Caoimghin displayed a strong patriotic outlook, inherited no doubt from both his parents whose families had been active in the national movement since Fenian times. A committed republican who adhered throughout his life to the ideals of the First Dáil Éireann, his patriotism manifested itself in a particular way in concern for the people of his native Mayo and of the west of Ireland generally.

In the 1950s, he was among those who established Coláiste Pádraig at Swinford to provide secondary education facilities for the boys of the neighbourhood. The college was staffed by priests of the Diocese of Achonry with some lay graduates to complement the work of the Mercy Sisters, who were already providing day and boarding facilities for girls. He was also involved in the erection of a scheme of cottages for elderly people.

During the 1960s, when there was growing concern at the depopulation of the western counties, he was one of the founders of the Defence of the West movement, which pioneered ideas for regional development which have since become widely accepted and borne remarkable fruit. It is interesting to recall that it was Caoimghin who secured his first appointment on a local paper for his neighbour, the late John Healy, who later became such a prominent champion of the western counties.

In the early 1970s, Caoimghin's desire to explore the benefits that co-operatives could bring to those earning their livelihood from agriculture and fishing led him to take a course at the celebrated Saint Francis Xavier University run by the Antigonish Movement in Nova Scotia.

Thirty years ago, Caoimghin moved his practice to Galway, where he resided for the rest of his life. The office that he opened in Dominick Street was the most informal of places and held a warm welcome for all who called regardless of the purpose of their visit. From here, Caoimghin became known the length and breadth of Connemara as 'the people's solicitor', not only an adviser and advocate of ability and integrity but a person of humanity, compassion and understanding. Over his years in Galway, several young lawyers served their apprenticeships in his office and learned from their master, not only the practice of law, but valuable lessons as well in its humane administration.

Caoimghin was a man of extraordinary gentleness and almost infinite patience, slow to criticise, always ready to encourage. The secret of his remarkable ability to relate to others appears to have been an innate Christianity that caused him to seek only the best in everyone he met. He was invariably in good spirits, great company and always a delight to meet. He had a mischievous sense of humour and, as someone who had never taken alcohol or smoked, he loved to relate an encounter he had with Michael D Higgins at a dinner one evening. 'I thought you were a total abstainer, Caoimghin,' said Michael teasing him, 'and here I see you enjoying a sherry trifle!'

'Ah yes, Michael,' retorted Caoimghin, 'but have you never heard of the legal maxim "*De minimis non curat lex*" ("The law takes no regard of trifles")?'

For Caoimghin, the law was essentially an instrument for attaining justice between citizen and citizen, and between citizen and state. He was seen at his best as an advocate in the District Court, the lowest level of the court system and the one most familiar to the ordinary citizen. This was his favourite role and here he brought to the service of his client the legal skills he had inherited from his father and the knowledge acquired in half a lifetime's experience in that forum. He always studied his brief meticulously, ascertaining the facts with great care and relating them to the applicable principles of law. His manner in court was invariably quiet and restrained. Even in cross-examining a difficult witness, he never raised his voice or altered his tone. He set out his client's case cogently and pressed it with no more than gentle insistence.

He was often brought to Dublin, generally in cases of particular sensitivity, and he seldom failed to secure a successful outcome for his client. Caoimghin was recognised and respected by colleagues and clients, by judges and gardaí, for his erudition and integrity. Had he been so disposed, his expertise in law could have earned him an affluent lifestyle. Instead he settled for an almost Franciscan simplicity, never acquired a residence of his own and, for many years, did not even enjoy the convenience of a car.

He had a passion for the Irish language and used it as often as he possibly could. Although he modestly disclaimed proficiency in its use, he was a fluent speaker and even wrote verses in Irish, of which he was quite proud. He did not promote the language aggressively, as some enthusiasts have been known to do, for such an attitude would have been totally foreign to his nature.

In failing health, Caoimghin retired from practice in 1999 to a small house in Shantalla where he continued to entertain his friends. He continued to visit the city where he had long become a familiar and popular figure. The occasion of his eightieth birthday the following year was, to his surprise and delight, marked by a wonderful gathering of family, colleagues and friends.

His death, on 14th April 2002, evoked tributes from far and wide in press and radio. A fellow Mayo man John Garavan, who had known him as a colleague and latterly as district judge for the Galway area, spoke for many when he praised him for all the good he had done for so many people over the years.

Caoimghin was waked in the house of his son Pádraic at Barna. The mourners at the Funeral Mass, celebrated in Irish in the chapel at Furbo, were led by his widow, Carmel, their children and grandchildren. Before and during mass, the chapel rang with the voices of singers and the music of melodeon, fiddle, guitar and bodhrán. The coffin, wrapped in the Tricolour and lead by a lone piper, was carried to the nearby Reilig Éanna at the top of a hill, appropriately named Barr an tSléibhe. After the committal prayers had been said, the entire fifteen mysteries of the Rosary were recited while the grave was filled with earth by relays of family and friends. His old comrade, Ruairi O'Brádaigh, President of Republican Sinn Féin, who delivered the graveside oration said, 'If Caoimghin has not gone to heaven there is no hope for any of us.'

One could scarcely find a more fitting place of rest for Caoimghin MacCathmhaoil than this tranquil spot close to Spiddal in the heart of his beloved Iar Connacht, overlooking Galway Bay and its islands that he had come to know so well.

Gerard Brady

INSIDE OUT

GERARD BYRNE

Kaiserstrasse in Frankfurt-am-Main runs down to the main railway station, the Haubtbahnhof, in the heart of the city. Being near what is, perhaps, the busiest railway station in Europe, the street itself is a busy one, with shops and hotels and other businesses catering to the thousands of tourists and commuters travelling daily to and from the station and, like in many other cities, the area surrounding the station is also home to the so-called seedier side of life. Social outcasts are the order of the day. Prostitutes, petty criminals, drug addicts and homeless people abound. All in all, it is the sort of street where people, for one reason or another, are anonymous. Many times I had been to and from the railway station without ever expecting to see someone I knew, much less see someone I knew sheltering in a doorway, wrapped in a blanket. Peter wasn't his real name. His real name, which he told me only once, was to become forever memorable to a young, naïve and largely ignorant Irishman.

I arrived in Frankfurt in the summer of 1977 bursting with excitement. I was coming to live and work in a vibrant, foreign city for at least a year. I had taken German at university, having never studied it at school, so now, at the end of my freshman year, I determined that the only way to avoid another embarrassing year of lectures and classes where I hadn't the remotest clue what was going on was to live for a time in Germany. I had to actually learn the language before I could concern myself with the niceties of perfecting my fluency! Having finally cut the apron strings, which, being the youngest, were slightly tighter around me, I was all grown up and ready to start a new life.

The language barrier was pretty tough at first. My trusty phrasebook was invaluable in helping me to gurgle out a question, but was completely useless when it came to trying to understand the response. Undaunted, I ploughed onwards and, in a matter of weeks, I had a place to live, a job, a social circle and I was the proud possessor of the obligatory legal residence permit. Certainly, in my social and working environment, I was the very essence of the proverbial fish out of water. However, I was young, Irish, legal and white. People everywhere could not have been nicer. They bent over backwards to help me. I was a sort of novelty I suppose and I revelled in it. How truly wonderful it was to stand out, to be different, to be an outsider!

I was having the time of my life. However, the main reason I was there was to learn German and even though, just by being there, I was making great strides, I reckoned I should have a slightly more academic approach and so, twice a week, I went to night classes. That's where I met Peter.

There was almost literally a world of cultures in one room. Most spoke practically no German and even less English. Except for one. He introduced himself simply as Peter from India. He appeared to be more or less my age and, though his German seemed even poorer than mine, his English was perfect. He politely explained that Peter wasn't his real name, but was the name he went by in Germany. He didn't venture what his real name was and so I didn't ask. What struck me most about Peter was his politeness. He was very softly spoken, had a beaming smile, deep, dark eyes that had just a hint of sadness about them and, even though he was totally friendly and affable, there was an instantly detectable sense of reserve.

Because we were younger than most of the rest, and because of our common language, we became instant classroom buddies. Outside the school, however, Peter was a much more reluctant buddy. Any offer by me to introduce him to my social circle or to enter in any way my world beyond the class was always politely, but resolutely, refused. Nor was I invited into his. For a long time I was puzzled by this. However, his refusals were always absolute and eventually I left well enough alone. We remained good friends, but only twice a week.

Because I regaled him with stories and anecdotes about the wonderful time I was having in Germany and about my life in general, Peter knew a lot about my world beyond the classroom. I knew nothing of his. He would often cryptically tell me that he had learned a great deal in Germany, but little else. In the face of his evasiveness, I tried to curb my curiosity.

Then, one evening, while waiting for a tram on Kaiserstrasse, I noticed something strange about the two cold and wet-looking men I saw huddled in blankets in a doorway. I knew one of them! As I approached, Peter looked up and when he saw the puzzled and shocked look on my face, he merely smiled softly, stood up and said, 'Don't worry.' Then he took me gently by the arm and led me to a tiny bedsit nearby. He had kept me out of his world but, because I had accidentally stumbled upon it, that night I was invited in.

Peter was born in Bombay. He was an only child who was brought up in relatively comfortable circumstances. His parents, like my own, were small shopkeepers. His life was pretty much mapped out. He would go on to university to study law and, when qualified, he would find, together with his parents, a suitable woman to marry and settle down with a family. Just after his eighteenth birthday, his parents died in an accident and, suddenly, a life plan didn't seem so clear anymore. He was alone, lost and bereft and he felt that his whole life was crumbling around him. He needed to get far away. It was on a spontaneous whim that he decided to go to Europe.

He arrived in Frankfurt on a visitor's visa. Germany was to be the first stopover on an extended trip to Europe. He booked himself into the first decent-looking, cheap hotel he came across, which was near the main railway station. He had never been so far away from home before, but Europe seemed like an exciting place full of promise.

He was glad he'd come. The dark cloud was already beginning to lift. It didn't lift far. Within a day, his bag with his passport, papers and all his money was stolen. He went to the police. He felt that they were quite unsympathetic, but he couldn't be sure. They kept calling him Peter! It wasn't his name. He didn't speak German and they could speak very little English. He left armed with some addresses but wasn't quite sure what they were for. He felt stupid and humiliated. He was an innocent abroad. He had literally nowhere to go. He had no idea how long it would take to have money wired from India, nor was he sure how to arrange it. He was in an alien country, a different culture, he didn't speak the language, he had no legal right to work and he had even lost his name. He was homeless in the most rapid and unexpected fashion, and he was terrified. He had seen hundreds of homeless people in India, but it had never once occurred to him that the prospect might face him. He was lost in every sense of the word.

Peter was forced to live for just two weeks on the street, in the doorways and alleys and little hidden places that surrounded the main thoroughfare of Kaiserstrasse. He had, through no obvious fault of his own, been thrust onto the fringes of society and it took little time for him to realise precisely what that meant. He was exposed in the most brutal and complete manner. His dark skin was not an advantage. He discovered quickly that skin colour is often the first port of call for racial prejudice. Even the marginalised community, which he had now joined, had its own hierarchical system. He was new, young, foreign, and couldn't even speak the language. He was at the very bottom of the pile. He didn't know the system. He didn't know that choosing a particular doorway was encroaching on someone else's territory. More than once, he was beaten and kicked. More often than not, he was thrown out of coffee shops and bars when he tried to buy a cup of coffee or some food with what little money he had. He learned the horror of having to scrounge for food. He was approached for drugs and with drugs. He was approached for sex by people who believed that he was selling it, and threatened with violence by some who wanted to take it for nothing. He was spat on, urinated on and verbally abused. He was physically sick on an almost constant basis, but especially when he was forced to beg for money. His background had trained him to regard beggars with total disdain. He had considered them as worthless, not meriting the slightest consideration and now he was one of them. There was no rest, no sleep, no comfort. It was the worst kind of nightmare, truly hell on earth. But it would have an effect on him that he wasn't prepared for.

One evening, after an eternity of just two weeks on the street, the nightmare ended as abruptly as it had begun. Franzisca came upon Peter hovering near the entrance to a coffee shop. He had learned by now not to go in. It was obvious to her that he was in a state of some distress. She addressed him, at first unsuccessfully, in German and then in perfectly fluent English. She took him inside and bought him some hot food. In her confident company, nobody bothered him, though the looks of disdain were all around. He shyly and nervously told her his story.

Franzisca was a living angel. She took him home,

where, for the first time in two weeks, he was able to wash himself clean. She gave him a warm bed for the night and the next day she went with him to sort out the money transfer, which he had been unable to do. She invited him to stay until the money came through and she suggested with just a hint of a smile that it might not be a bad idea for him to learn German. She was a translator by profession but, twice a week, she gave a German language class at a nearby Volkshochschule, an adult education centre.

His new funds arrived shortly after and, with Franzisca's help, he rented a small flat. He knew that the wisest thing now would be to return home, but something was stopping him. While strolling around his old neighbourhood seeing familiar faces, who didn't recognise the young man who shortly before was a temporary member of their fold, he realised that, apart from India, this was the only other corner of the world that he knew, that he knew intimately, that he knew better than most Germans. He hadn't had the opportunity to venture beyond the Kaiserstrasse district, and it suddenly struck him with an unexpected clarity that, for now, it was where he belonged.

Peter had spent two weeks living from the inside out. He spent the next few months living from the outside in. He used funds from home to help what he now considered his adopted community. He took Franzisca's German classes to help him communicate. He brought people food. He bought them blankets. He kept them company. If they couldn't go into a coffee shop or bar, he wouldn't either. Sometimes, he gave one of them a bed for the night in his flat. Sometimes, he slept rough with the more vulnerable ones. He paid for hostels, he paid for clothes. His two German classes were his only venture into the outside world. Any other social life would have made him lose focus and, besides, it would have eaten into precious funds and precious time. Peter knew that this was all only temporary, for him and for them. It wasn't meant to solve problems; it was meant to ease pain. It was from the heart, not the head. He wasn't trying to change the world, he was just a young stranger, now at home, showing a little compassion and trying to make life a little easier for a very few people. But, in his soul, he believed that coming to Europe hadn't been a whim after all. He believed that it was meant to be. The cruelty of rejection had taught him how truly horrific it could be to stand out, to be different, to be an outsider.

During a very brief period in his life, Peter came to know that, being social animals, we tend to look for safety in numbers. Conforming to a social norm helps us to maintain our social worth and we reinforce this by identifying difference in some, which enables us to exclude them. But all people are affected in their lifetime by all the things that happen in their world – big things and small things, good experiences and bad, a kick or a kindness. Nobody is an exception to this general rule. We are all the same because we are all different and this is what makes us great. Peter didn't change the world in any tangible way. He didn't become a great humanitarian, or a Nobel laureate, or a champion of social injustice. He went back to India and simply carried on with his life. But Peter himself was changed and that is just as significant. He had an effect on me that I have never forgotten and, like the ripples in a lake when a stone is thrown in, imagine the number of people he has touched since.

And imagine if we were all like that. That same night, Peter told me his real name.

Gerard Byrne

A VOICE FROM OUTSIDE

CATHERINE CLEARY AND RICHARD OAKLEY

It was a bad day to be adrift in Dublin. The pavements were crowded with happy families as people lined up to watch the St Patrick's Day parade. It was the 1980s on O'Connell Street. In the middle of the throng, a homeless teenager from Wexford ached for family and home.

Colm O'Gorman picked up a public phone and dialled his old number. He had no money for the call so he could just hear his brother's voice through the beeps, 'Hello... hello...' Then the receiver died.

Colm had been ill that day and was just wandering around. It helped just listening to his brother even though he couldn't be heard. It was his lowest 'conscious' moment. There had been many more wretched and desperate ones, in the months he spent on the streets.

There were days when he would lock himself into a toilet cubicle in Burger King on O'Connell Street and try to sleep sitting on the toilet. There was a bush in a park in Ranelagh he slept under. Sometimes, he would be picked up for the night. It meant a bed, but it also meant having sex with someone. He was so disconnected at the time that he was unaware of how terrifying the existence he was living was.

But that St Patrick's Day was the moment when Colm felt utterly alone. He was walking around in his own bubble, surrounded by people enjoying the Catholic Church's and the country's national day of celebration.

Now, nearly two decades later, Colm O'Gorman is one of the most-respected and authoritative voices on the issue of sexual abuse. The voiceless boy on a public phone with no money has become one of the clearest voices for thousands of people. Some of whom had remained silent for decades about their abuse.

Finding that voice has been a long journey, starting with the loss of himself at the hands of his abuser, Fr Sean Fortune. He can pinpoint vividly the moment when it happened.

One morning in his bedroom, Colm almost told his mother what the respected and feared Fr Fortune was doing to him. The priest was waiting downstairs, having called to his home in Wexford to take him away for the weekend. It was the second or third such trip and Colm, then fifteen years old, knew that a weekend of rape and abuse was ahead.

All he could tell his mother was that he did not want to go. He kept trying to tell her why but he couldn't. At that time, the language didn't exist for him to do so and, with the voice of Fortune in his head telling him he had a problem, he felt telling his mother would have meant confessing something he was doing as much as anything else.

Fortune fed the self-loathing and guilt of his victims, convincing them they were to blame for his crimes. For the fifteen-year-old boy struggling to tell his mother in his bedroom that morning, it was like being in a pool hanging on to the edge, hanging on and hanging on. When he couldn't get the words out, he felt as if he'd just let go of the edge. He let go and drowned.

After the old Colm floated away, he felt as if he was leading two lives; a good son, a good friend, a good whatever. The worse the abuse became, the more he became a people pleaser, the more he hid what was happening to him.

The abuse continued until Colm was seventeen. He had finished his Leaving Cert and was planning to study hotel management at Cathal Brugha Street. However, his move to college was on hold as he was trying to find the money to go. Then Fortune offered him £300 to find someone else – younger than Colm – that Fortune could abuse, and that was the last straw. Within six weeks, in January 1984, he had packed a suitcase and hitched a lift to Dublin. At first, he bedded down with friends in a house in Crumlin and then he drifted, severely depressed, onto the streets.

Six months later, his sister Barbara found him. By then he was working in a restaurant beside the Olympia Theatre in the city centre and was sharing a house. He went to Maynooth with her, where she was attending college. Still blaming himself for what had happened at the hands of Fortune, he tried to tell her what had happened but ended up telling her he had had an affair with the priest. The memory of that phrase still makes him wince today.

He told her that he was gay and left the next day. His sister told his brother and they both told his father, who Colm simply couldn't face. For years, his relationship with his father had been fractured beyond repair. Colm blamed himself and was frightened his dad would see him as the disgusting freak that he believed himself to be. He felt he didn't deserve to be on good terms with his father.

For the next two years, life improved. He made good friends and found a sense of community in the city's gay scene. However, his past remained unconfronted and bundled up inside. He was on his feet, but still had a distance to travel.

On a whim, he decided he was getting nowhere in Dublin and went to England. He left behind his new friends, moved further away from Wexford and from his family, but he brought his problems with him.

In England, he drifted from one job to the next, mainly working in the service industry. He became a restaurant manager in a hotel in Bath but then quit because he still felt he had no right to be successful.

Eventually, he made the decision that would be the start of a huge change in his life. In 1994, he started to train and then work as a physical therapist. He started to think about wellbeing and health and, for the first time, began to look at himself.

Wexford was not far from his thoughts and word reached him of a family wedding due to take place at home where Fortune was to be the celebrant. His father did not want to go, but his sister reported back that Fortune was there with a crowd of teenagers around him.

His first thought was to send a letter to the bishop. He now says it was ironic that, ten years out of Wexford, the old habits of Church teaching were still engrained.

But thinking about Fortune had opened old wounds. On New Year's Eve that year, Colm pulled his sister and one of his friends into a room and broke down, telling them everything. To get through it, he had to face his biggest fear – he had to talk to his father. Within a month, he had returned to Wexford.

It was not easy. Colm found it difficult to talk about what had happened. His father found it hard to separate what had happened to Colm from his son's sexuality. The confrontation brought both men closer than they had ever been in their lives. Colm still has a picture taken at home of his father in his overalls, home early from work to see his son off.

During that week, Colm spent days making statements to the gardaí about Fortune. His reconciliation with his father happened just in time. Ten months later, his father was diagnosed with terminal cancer.

Back in London, Colm sought out a counsellor. Now he sees that he was still skimming the surface. He went to a counsellor 'to be okay' rather than to actually deal with the abuse. It was two years before he 'hit the crisis' that then prompted him to train as a psychotherapist.

It was through this training that Colm reclaimed himself from his abuse. To his ears, it's hard not to sound 'so bloody Californian' when he starts to talk about it.

But he found he learned how to create a space into which he could emerge. He realised that his past was not his fault. He sees himself now as neither a victim nor a survivor, but someone who experienced sexual abuse and got beyond it. 'I'm really beginning to glory in that. We are all magnificent and wonderful and amazing and very ordinary people.'

Now Colm O'Gorman creates the same space for other people. He established the organisation One in Four in London in 1999 after coming together with like-minded counsellors. The organisation gets its name from the number of people that are estimated to suffer some kind of abuse.

As part of his work with One in Four, Colm took an abuse case in Britain to the BBC and began working on a documentary with producer Sarah McDonald. Slowly, he told her his own story and, after a little persuasion, she convinced him it would be a compelling documentary.

Just how compelling, Colm could never have realised. The programme, *Suing the Pope*, changed two lives for ever: the boy who fled Wexford as a teenager with a suitcase and one of the most powerful men in the Irish Catholic Church, Bishop Brendan Comiskey. The power of television hit home in a way that no coverage about the abuse in the Ferns Diocese had done, and Comiskey resigned his post.

Now strangers congratulate Colm on the street, people ring him all the time and he has received awards for his work, which he thinks is far from over. When he picks up the phone now, people listen. Those people are in positions of real power, right up to the Taoiseach's office itself.

On a personal level, Colm O'Gorman is still affected by what happened in Wexford when he was a teenager. As part of the process of getting himself back, he has returned to places and things he had to run away from. He is back working with people, as he wanted to do when he was a teenager in Wexford. He is back working in Dublin and says he won't leave Ireland 'ever again'.

He is even looking to build a house in Wexford with his partner. In his own words, he describes it as a reconciliation and a homecoming. Colm O'Gorman has come home to himself.

Catherine Cleary and Richard Oakley

DR NANCY DUNNE: CLINICAL ECOLOGIST

MARY CONDREN

When did a doctor last ask you about the water you drink? The chemical additives or preservatives in your food? The quality of air in your home or workplace? How well your body digests your food? What has this got to do with the status of outsider? A great deal, as it happens.

Social theorists consider that we have paid a high price for being civilised. We have had to swap a natural relationship with our animal bodies for an unhealthy splitting off from our physical selves, the willingness to be associated only with our healthy, pleasant physicality, not with our unsightly, unwell or unpleasant skin, odours and excretions. The result? The parts of ourselves we reject, we project on to others. We deal with this 'stranger' inside us by dispelling it into the 'stranger outside'.

By rejecting or ignoring our own bodies, we help create the outsiders in our own societies. Anyone who represents the possible chaos into which we may descend – the mentally ill, homeless, disabled – serves as a warning to us, effectively policing, disciplining and forming our precarious identities.

But what turns someone into an outsider? In some cases, tragedy, fate, illness and misfortune all play a role. The outsider becomes the watchdog for normalcy; a living warning against complacency; a living testament to failure. Take the homeless: sitting and drinking and setting up house on the streets, reminding us of who or what we might become, if we are not careful – if we don't look after ourselves.

Even doctors can become outsiders. Those doctors and healers who insist on honouring our body wisdom, who look at nails and skin and tongue, at whites of eyes, who ask questions about the ways we live our daily lives, like detectives looking for clues to a deeper mystery, these healers are often expelled, ridiculed and/or excluded by their colleagues or the medical establishment. They are not admitted to the places where the dominant social and professional practices carry out their work.

One such professional outsider was Irishwoman Dr Nancy Dunne MB, BCh (NUI), buried in March 2003 in a small Wicklow graveyard, surrounded by a circle of family and friends, at the end of a long and courageous journey – adventure of life – in which she pioneered a path for which many of us can be forever grateful. Many Irish people owe their health, and sometimes sanity, to her life's work.

Born in Kilternan, County Dublin, Nancy Gleeson graduated at the top of her class (a Gold Medallist) and became the first woman registrar in the Mater Misericordiae Hospital in 1949. Positions in England and Ireland followed but, like many women of her generation, she ceased her active practice on the birth of her first child.

Dr Dunne was always a writer but was too passionate about her medical-practice work to spend time at her desk. Ironically, it was only in her final years when she became blind that she put pen to paper and started to tell her story, a story that will hopefully soon be published.

Here our question is this: how did such a promising professional become an outsider? Let's turn back to the questions at the beginning.

During her medical training, Nancy had a sense that she was being trained to treat the symptoms, not the causes of illness. She often spoke of her mother and her Great Aunt Lizzie, natural healers in their own time.

She regretted not paying attention as a child when her aunt would take her into the fields and forests picking herbs and flowers to make concoctions that she would take to the local families with TB, cancer and other serious and 'incurable' illnesses of that time. Like her foresisters, Nancy wanted to learn about trusting the body's innate wisdom, listening to its voice, seeing its symptoms and signs as precious clues to what was wrong, and trusting its capacity to heal with nature's resources.

In 1984, her children raised, she resumed her medical practice. However, she immediately saw a massive change in the illnesses presented to her, especially the incidences of allergic illness, hyperactivity, digestive and even mental disorders. She knew something was radically wrong.

Like the ancient healers before her, she started with the four elements: water, air, earth and fire. If the most basic constituent elements of the body were assaulted, good health could not prevail. She looked for explanations: contamination of the drinking water and the soil, the widespread use of antibiotics, nutritionally depleted fast-food diets, pollution of the air. Dr Dunne believed that such abuse had widespread consequences for future generations.

To the memories of her mother and aunt she now turned, and found their wisdom embodied in a medical approach that, in the coming years, would increasingly gain credence: clinical ecology. Clinical ecologists consider the human body, and especially the immune system, to be breaking down under the weight of the pollution generated, in particular, by Western society. The children of chemically contaminated and nutritionally exhausted parents enter life seriously compromised. Often only massive nutritional interventions can stabilise their biochemistries, enabling them to live relatively normal lives. This emerging discipline, orthomolecular medicine, Dr Dunne embraced wholeheartedly; indeed, she was passionate about it.

Its principal tenets are simple: if the doctors of to-day don't become the nutritionists of tomorrow, then the nutritionists of today will be the doctors of tomor-row. In this, clinical ecologists are making their way back to the abject neglected body, the one so totally taken for granted by all of us until it collapses under the weight of our own abuse.

For the last twenty years of her life, Dr Dunne de-voted her time to researching and networking with pro-fessionals around the globe, treating those patients who came to her (often as a last resort) from all over Ireland and indeed Europe. Naturally, her first questions con-cerned the air they breathed, the foods they ate, the water they drank and how they burned the fuel within.

Dr Dunne could have told many horror stories of the diet sheets she collected. (She insisted that intend-ing patients record their daily intake of food and drink (including alcohol) for two weeks before she saw them.) She often marvelled at how people survived at all with no real food whatsoever from week to week. 'It stands to reason,' she would often say, 'if you fed rats on diets like that, they would kill each other.'

Doctors told of patients being admitted to psychiat-ric hospitals. Challenged to try out their theories on them, the first thing orthomolecular doctors gave these pa-tients was a diet sheet. A famous case recorded was that of a young girl who admitted to drinking twenty-four cans of Coke per day before becoming psychotic. Not only were these patients abusing their bodies with false food (empty calories), but they were also filling them-selves up, so that the natural wisdom of the body (hun-ger pangs) had no chance of kicking in with the warn-ing signs.

Other patients became psychotic when exposed to

unventilated mobile gas heaters. Her patients, she considered, were like hapless canaries in the mine.

Such patients signalled to her the dangers of com-
promising the health of future generations by not paying attention to the warning signs and adapting our living habits accordingly. She described how a child presenting with an allergy to (for instance) cow's milk, indi-
cated a 'third-generation allergy'; a young adult person
presenting with the same, 'a second-generation allergy';
and an adult in later life, 'a first-generation allergy'.

In her practice, children were a priority. Often reared
on chemically contaminated foods, sensitivity to chemical additives and preservatives started to become a widespread problem. Extreme behavioural problems meant
many children were considered 'bad' or 'troubled' or
even mentally deficient. These were her most reward-
ing cases.

She recalled one eight-year-old boy who exhibited
violent behaviour when he had eaten the wrong foods.
He had serious problems at home and in school. After
one session in her surgery where he listened to Dr Dunne
explaining to his mother what hyperactivity was and how
all of his classic behavioural symptoms were attribut-
able to this disease, they got up to leave. The young
child reached out his hand to her and shook it heartily
saying, 'Thanks very much Dr Dunne', with a serious-
ness older than his years. At last someone understood
that he couldn't help his bizarre and erratic behaviour.

For seven years, she worked anonymously in Recovery, an organisation aimed at the prevention of mental
illness, where she trained group leaders and formed self-
help groups – and where she insisted that nobody knew
she was a doctor. This was kept a secret until the day
she left, when she felt she had given all the knowledge
that she could give. She also worked with alcoholics on
the assumption that their blood sugar was imbalanced,

that they were greatly depleted in the B vitamins, and often suffered other serious biochemical abnormalities that were never investigated, let alone diagnosed.

Among orthomolecular doctors, many studies have taken place on the diets of those who found themselves incarcerated in institutions. Other studies detail the behavioural reversals possible when wholesome foods and corrective nutrition have been prescribed.

Dr Dunne believed in the intimate link between delinquent behaviour and food allergy or intolerance (inability to process certain foods). Many potential delinquents in Ireland owe their 'ordinary' lives to her intervention and research.

She was a founder member, in the 1970s, of the Irish Allergy Treatment and Research Association and the Hyperactive Society in the UK. She devised healthy and palatable recipes, gave public lectures, conducted clinics and dealt with thousands of postal requests from all over Europe. Even in the last several years, when, clinically blind, she had retired to Wicklow, she held seminars for groups of up to twelve health professionals at a time, dedicated to carrying on her work.

She won many awards abroad for her papers on hypoglycaemia (low blood sugar), the effects of light on health, fungal poisons in cereal and food and chemical allergies. She was appointed an honorary director of the American National Board of Psychiatry for her contributions to the prevention of mental illness. She entered briefly into the public arena in Ireland in the mid-1970s with an article on a subject dear to her heart: 'The Use of Injected and Sublingual Urine in the Treatment of Allergies'.

Traditional healers in many countries had long used urine in the treatment of various illnesses, with great effect. Dr Dunne had good reason to believe that homeopathic sublingual doses of a patient's own urine could be used to boost immune function and aid in recovery from allergic illness. Promising research had begun in the US treating patients with HIV/Aids. Given the appalling vistas now opening up, where whole continents could be wiped out with the spread of Aids, any potentially inexpensive solutions should at least be investigated. It goes without saying that no funding was forthcoming from the pharmaceutical companies: urine is free; patents would be ridiculous.

Dr Dunne published two articles in the *Irish Medical Times* calling for funds and resources to be allocated to this emerging field of research. However, it was one thing for the medical establishment to tolerate someone who dealt with their hopeless cases, it was something else to tolerate her calling for research funds. And for urine? The scathing response of her medical colleagues was predictable.

When the second article was published, just one of her staunch female colleagues wrote to the *Irish Medical Times* to request that any criticism be directed toward the topic and not at the person suggesting the hypothesis. Thankfully, however, before her death Dr Dunne was thrilled to find that two international seminars on urine therapy had been held and that her research will eventually bear fruit.

However, from that point on in Ireland, she maintained a very low profile, refusing to appear on television, speak on radio or to be interviewed in the papers. She shunned publicity, but gave freely of her work and insights to other health professionals, some of whom quickly went into print gaining the credit (and remuneration) that should rightly have been hers.

But credit, fame, money – none of these concerned her. She embraced her status as an outsider: she often described herself as a 'round peg in a square hole', and never gave up trying to make a difference. But she grieved when the vulnerable went untreated, given the narrowness of approach fostered by the powerful dominant assumptions of Western medicine.

Modern medicine, far from helping us to make friends with our bodies, contributes to our alienation. We no longer trust our bodies with their inherent wisdom and ability to heal. We do not listen when they are speaking by way of symptoms, we do not rest when we are tired. Even when our bodies speak the loudest (in dreams and nightmares) we ignore this rich goldmine of information in favour of scientific and technical abstractions – just like putting in ear plugs to block out our body's inner voice of wisdom.

As symptoms indicate to us where things have gone wrong in our bodies, social delinquents indicate to us where our society has gone wrong and where we need to concentrate resources to bring society back into balance. It is interesting to note that when a delinquent was identified in ancient Native American cultures, that person was 'sentenced' to spend one year with the tribal elders, something we would consider an honour. It was understood that the person who had committed an offence needed more, not less, spiritual and social guidance. The outsider was embraced, not shunned.

Dr Nancy Dunne knew that, as her mentor Dr Abram Hoffer, once said, 'It only takes one to make a difference.' She might not have chosen her status as outsider, but she embraced that status when it came. The alternative was unthinkable: to abdicate the findings of her intelligence, the fruits of her medical practice or the mighty weight of her own integrity.

Mary Condren

TYPESCRIPT

OLIVER CONNOLLY

There was a name and a date of birth and an address that changed frequently between a small number of very familiar places – and always the bag. Sometimes weekend, sometimes plastic. He had the humour and persistence but, in his case, there was an abiding courtesy, which was constant even at the darkest hour.

His refinement aroused a certain curiosity but I never enquired of him or of any of the others. He moved alone, but he knew the others and they knew him, as their paths crisscrossed over the years in that curious fellowship, where from time to time they had to live at close quarters. There were house rules but there were other more important rules, foremost of which was the sanctity of the personal past. It had been a long retreat that had led to that sort of peace. There were small triumphs and sideshows along the way but they always lost ground, and it had taken a long and difficult time to accept that this was life as it was going to be. This acceptance led to a certain calm, an equanimity, as long as the past was left out.

Over the years, he revealed unsolicited glimpses, a new vignette every year. I see a photograph that hung in a rectory hallway. It is in a sepia frame with foxed mount entitled 'Dublin univ second XI 1937'. Young men in white flannels, they look middle-aged. There he is in the second row, third from the left, between Trotter and Nunn. 'In Modern Languages'. Majoring in German, he spent his summers in the Reich and made many good friends there. But there is no graduation photograph.

It is summer 1940, and the cricket flannels have been changed for a flying officer's uniform and life jacket. Influence had been exerted to get him into fighter com-

mand. When he first arrived, he was surprised to be
regarded as a 'Paddy' and was not totally accepted in the
officers' mess. But, by early August, it was almost emp-
tied by casualties who had to be quickly replaced by ser-
geants. Not only was he still there, but 'Paddy' was dis-
tinguishing himself in his Spitfire with many hits day
after day, high over the home counties of England.

Hits involved firing his 8 Browning machine guns in
short bursts of 3,200 bullets into Messerschmitt
BF109Es manned by young Germans. These were the
Germans with whom he had spent his enjoyable summers before the war. He had learned to tune in on their
radio wavelength and listen to them, he understood what
they were saying and continued to listen after they had
been hit.

By the middle of September, the Luftwaffe had
stopped attacking fighter command. The pressure was
over – he had survived what came to be called the Battle of Britain and received his medals. He had been par-
tially deafened by his own machine guns, but had received no other injuries. For the rest of the war, he was
on air force radio intelligence because of his knowledge of German. But, when peace was declared, it did
not apply to him. It was the voices, the voices he had
heard in his earphones from the Messerschmitts that
were going down. They stayed with him. Various at-
tempts at an ordinary life failed.

The voices had seen to that. Alcohol reduced the
volume somewhat. Furthermore, the volume of the
voices was inversely proportional to the volume of alcohol. He gradually joined the fellowship.

The years and the anecdotes mounted up.

It is sunset at the Simon Community and a figure
rings the shelter bell. There follows a brief consultation
with a man in shirtsleeves carrying a bunch of keys. The
girl in the office announces that alcohol is not allowed

on the premises. 'Is that a bottle that I see in your pocket?' She braces herself for a tirade. He produces a full bottle of whiskey and hands it over, bowing politely and saying with a smile, 'You are quite right, my dear.'

In Johnson's Court, he plays Moore's Melodies on the concert flute. The standard of the music is almost professional. With the melodies, comes money.

The manager of an expensive hotel rings. He is worried about a man. He has a concert flute and large amounts of cash. He has been staying at the hotel for months. He pays cash in advance.

He has so much cash that the manager follows him to his room every evening collecting cash that falls from his pockets.

I visit him and he smiles and tells me that he plays the flute for his own enjoyment. He is trying to get it perfect. If you play a musical instrument in public because you have no place of your own in which to play, people put money at your feet. But money was no use because the voices were still there.

There were times when the bottle triumphed. For serious drinking, solitude was necessary.

The voice of the hostel superintendent on the telephone explained that one of the men had been in his room for three weeks. Nobody had seen him but he was in there. Somehow, he had managed to get drink in. Nobody knew how. They could hear him in there. They were going to have to use the master key. Could I come over?

I am led through great passages, past many tiny doors. In his minimalist room, and unaware of any crisis, he is serene and charming, but uncertain of time and not quite sure of place. The superintendent is greeted like an old friend, whose name he cannot quite remember. I accept further warm greetings. We exchange pleasantries. I eventually explain that it would best if he slipped away quietly. He seems surprised and, furthermore, there was no place to which he could slip.

Two days later, I received the expected phone call. Because of the commotion in the background, I had difficulty in recognising the superintendent's voice. There had been trouble and the man I visited was leaving the hostel. The police were in the hall. He would hold up the telephone to give me some idea of what was happening. The commotion continued and then a familiar voice said simply 'gosh'.

More years go by, more hostels and more shelters. We are in regular contact. The buildings have been improved and modernised, but the residents seem to stay the same – now the superintendent has a mobile phone and we go up in a lift. He gives me directions to the room. The old courtesies prevail. I am struck by the number of radios in the room, on the floor, on the locker and on the bed. I assume they are for music. No, no, they are for, *Deutsche Welle*, the German-language world service on shortwave. Then I knew. The voices were still there. I felt I could now ask what the voices from the Messerscumitts had been saying. '*Mutter*,' he said, 'they had been calling for their mothers. It was always the same, always *Mutter*.'

As I was leaving he was trying another radio for *Deutsche Welle*.

Several months passed and I had not seen him until one of the fellowship called to tell me that he had died. He had gone from hostel to hospice and the voices were silent at last.

Oliver Connolly

A TREASURED RECOLLECTION

BERNADETTE CRONIN

'There is no such thing as can't, there is nothing impossible.' This was a piece of advice slung, arrow style, into my brain on a warm sunny May day back in the late 1950s by Sr Mary Bridget, or 'Budge' as she was affectionately known to her students at Presentation Convent, in Bandon, County Cork. She finished the *n't* in 'can't' in a crescendo and hissed the word 'nothing'.

The incident arose after I had been dozing, happily and idly, at a desk positioned near the back of the classroom. I leaned back comfortably, where I was well supported by the partition, in an ideal position to gain maximum benefit from the heat of the sun, as it shafted through the giant Georgian classroom windows. My friend, Eileen, my desk mate for maths class, was also enjoying a restful and reclining pose. I was always careful to select a desk that got maximum sunrays, as it relieved the gloom of the classrooms.

In my blissful state of idle-mindedness, I noticed how the sun turned the tiny circle of my newly acquired signet ring into a spotlight. Signet rings were a deadly fashionable 'must have' of the times. I noticed it reflected like a white spot on the blackboard and elbowed Eileen to observe my discovery. She instantly grasped the prospects of the discovery and tried to stifle what would normally have been, for her, an explosion of laughter. She readily anticipated the next move as I guided the spot on to Sr Brigid's veil gradually moving towards her spectacles. By this time, both of us were becoming intoxicated with the tension of the next move as I directed the spot straight to her eyeball. She sprang from the step up to the blackboard and shot straight in my direction, hand extended, fuming at the audacity of one of her laziest maths students.

'Give me that, and get up to the board and do that algebra exercise I have been doing for the last half hour!' she snapped at me, as I parted with my prize possession.

I moved faster than usual towards the board. I fooled around a bit with as and xs and ys and even dared to glance at my friend, who, by now, had transformed to a near saintly expression of all consuming interest. Of course, I had been oblivious to the fact that sister had moved from geometry to algebra and, anyway, I had a general ambivalence to the subject. Eventually, feeling that I had wasted enough time out of the warmth of the sun, I ventured an 'I can't, Sister', following which she delivered the words that remained indelibly imprinted in my mind.

She was different. She didn't just enter a classroom to teach subjects to a motley crew of teenage girls who came from backgrounds that spanned the entire social and economic spectrum. She came to infuse into our minds and souls a desire for knowledge, the possession of which she believed brought in its wake an inevitable feeling of self worth. For her it was an uphill battle that she must often have felt like abandoning in dismay. 'Girls you can do it. The boys' schools do honours maths,' she would normally say, adding in a whispered mumble, 'and so should our school', when we expressed reservations or exaggerated difficulties with maths problems, just to waste class time. In hindsight, she was right. Many of us were not sufficiently challenged during the class due to the gender-based discriminatory attitudes prevailing in education at the time.

There was an economic depression in post Second World War Ireland, a war that was still being spoken of as though it had just stopped the year before. This was a time when tigers, Celtic or otherwise, were only associated with the annual school outing to Dublin Zoo. These were the times when girls, generally, were advised and primed to be good future housewives, nurses and teachers and, for a privileged few, 'The Bank' that, allegedly, accelerated a girl's marriage prospects in the right financial direction.

Thus, the mandatory inclusion of domestic science in the curriculum of most girls' schools seemed to get the word 'science' inserted somewhere and muzzle the would-be troubleshooters of the female persuasion, those who might be inclined to make further financial demands on an already famished government coffer. Sister Brigid, nevertheless, cajoled, coaxed and warned us to 'wake up' and realise that, by going that extra yard, workwise, university was an option. She pursued us with the same vigour in the subject of Latin, whilst at the same time bemoaning the fact that French was not taught in our school, despite her degree in French, which caused her open anguish for our sakes. The Latin was included, no doubt, in the unlikely event that we girls might be required to 'answer' the Latin Rite Mass – outside the altar rails of course. However, she begged of us to learn it and desperately tried to create an atmosphere of interest around Virgil's *Aeneid*, in a vain hope that we would sit the Matriculation Examination and get into UCC.

The exclusion of French and honours maths from our daily regime did not sit well with Sr Brigid. She implored us to keep UCC to the forefront of our minds. She knew that we as girls, the future women of this country and the world, were being deprived of routes open mainly to the male of the species. Few at the time ventured past those boundaries.

Her dogged determination to get through our disinterested skulls and into our brain that the barriers we perceived were false, a mere illusion to dupe us, remained stuck somewhere in the caverns of our minds. If we but pushed the boundaries out that little bit, we, the entire class, could all be in university, and a wonderful world of opportunity would open up to us. We would be unstoppable in our achievements.

Her passion and zeal for our welfare couldn't be hidden behind her sometimes rather stern rebukes at our misconduct. Her tolerance and understanding of our youthful nonsense always emerged at the conclusion of the class. She would allow a flicker of a smile as she gathered her books and shook her head in a gesture of feigned despair – 'Oh girls, what will I do with you all?' she would say, as she exited the classroom.

She prayed with the same intensity before each class, which was always another source of amusement to us. She closed her eyes and emphasised each aspiration in a way that could not be misunderstood for anything other than deep spiritual humility and sincerity.

Sister Mary Bridget was herself inspired by Nano Nagle, founder of the Presentation Order.

Nano Nagle was born in 1718 to a well-off farming family, in a place called Ballygriffin in County Cork. She could well have pursued a pleasant lifestyle in the manner of her kind at the time. However, she was born at a time when the infamous Penal Laws were enforced in Ireland to crush the Catholic population, and to deprive them of any education at all. Hedge-schools sprung up all over the country but brave teachers and parents conspired to outwit the oppressive anti-Catholic system of the day. Nano attended a hedge-school during her formative years, and then continued her education in France, an indication of her family's social status. Following the completion of her formal education, she lived a very pleasant, moderately high-society lifestyle around Paris amongst the intelligentsia and other privileged Irish émigrés of the time. She became restless.

Visions of an oppressed and persecuted people, her people, plummeting towards rampant illiteracy and worse, poverty, drew her back home to Cork. Thus, she stepped through the illusory door of fear, to become an outsider in the female world of her day.

At the age of thirty-four, she defied the system, the authorities of the day, even risking imprisonment or worse, and opened her first school for the miserably poor in Cork city. On Christmas Eve 1775, Nano Nagle, in the company of three other Cork women of like mind, the Misses Mary Ann Collins, Mary Fouhy and Elizabeth Bourke, founded the Congregation of Sisters of the Presentation, and became the first of what we always called the 'Pres Nuns'.

Encouraged by her, schools sprang up in the south and north sides of the city and, having started an unstoppable trend, she died a mere decade following the founding of her order. She was relatively young, in today's terms, at sixty-seven years, proof positive – as if proof were needed – that time or age should never be cited as a reason for the non-pursuit of a project motivated by a true and genuine spirit to improve the lot of one's fellow human beings.

Legend has it that Nano Nagle, accompanied by a small band of her sisters in religion, headed for Bandon in West Cork, to open a convent school there. Today, that trip is a mere twenty minutes' drive but then, no doubt, it was a long and awkward journey. However, the nuns confirmed that it was in 1829, forty-four years after Nano's death, that a West Cork woman called Catherine O'Neill, fortified financially by her mother's personal fortune, built the Presentation Convent in Bandon. The story goes that, from the moment they alighted from their means of transport, dressed in their religious garb – headdress obvious, rosaries dangling by their sides –

they were jeered, booed and worse by hostile towns-people each step of their way en route to the convent on the top of the hill on the outskirts of the town. That hill has since been known as Convent Hill.

History confirms that such events merely whetted the nuns' appetite for success in the world of minds and souls. Down all the decades, now centuries, pupils of all religious persuasion, and none, have reaped the rewards that emanated from the inheritance so gener-ously bequeathed by Nano Nagle and her faithful con-gregation. Sister Mary Brigid, she was a true daughter of Nano Nagle, and not all of what she said that warm May day was lost.

Bernadette Cronin

NAZMA'S STORY

Bangladesh was once described by Henry Kissinger as 'a basket case', while the international aid agencies have a tendency, in a words of one Bangladeshi I met, to 'present us as miserable and up to our knees in water'. However, everything about Bangladesh surprised me: the place, the people and, most of all, Nazma Aktor.

I had gone there with Ronan Tynan to make a film documentary about what life is like for the hundreds of thousands of mostly women and young girls who work in the sweat shops and export factories of the country's garment industry – the mainstay of the economy. But, from the moment we arrived, it was obvious the highly negative image of the place and the people, almost accepted without question by many in the so-called First World, is wide of the mark.

The Bangladesh we encountered is a country where the people are incredibly hardworking and show extraordinary enterprise in making a living, often against the odds and in the face of very challenging environmental and climatic conditions. For us, no one personified that outgoing and confident side of Bangladesh more than Nazma Aktor, a striking woman and a fearless trade-union leader in a conservative Muslim society, where the pecking order was aptly summed up for me by one observer as, 'Men, boys and women in that order!'

I first met Nazma on a blisteringly hot day with the temperatures well above 40 degrees centigrade – a heat wave in a country where the average summer temperatures are well above what most Irish people ever experience. The enterprise and resilience of the Bangladeshis was brought to light for me following Nazma, almost five months pregnant, as she went about her hectic daily schedule.

To put Nazma in some kind of context for readers, it is probably fair to say that she would have more in common with James Larkin in the early part of the twentieth century when trade unions were not recognised. Workers, who sought to fight for better wages and conditions, were fired and blacklisted, and had to take great risks on behalf of their fellow workers.

Like Larkin's fellow trade unionists, most of Nazma's members live in appalling slum conditions, which we visited and filmed first hand — although it is very difficult to convey what life is really like trying to bring up a family in a one-room shack, in a sprawling slum, with a corrugated-iron roof and no sanitation in extreme tropical temperatures. The remarkable nature of the Bangladeshis was constantly brought home to me seeing them emerge everyday from their very basic slum dwellings always immaculately turned out.

Nazma works very long hours and can often be found in her office well after midnight, meeting her members who can only visit her at very unsocial hours because they are often forced to work up to twelve hours a day, and sometimes even overnight in the factories when rush orders must be met. But the main grievance of the women workers who come to Nazma night after night, and one which quite shocked me given the very low wages they receive, is that they are often not paid on time.

It may seem barely credible when the workers in the sweat shops and the export factories live on the very margins of survival for as little as 8 cent an hour that they are not even paid on time, sometimes weeks or even months late. In fact, their bargaining position is so weak that, with economic conditions extremely poor at the moment and no other jobs prospect anywhere, they are reduced to simply fighting to be paid on time.

Nazma told me that when she started her trade-union activities, she was often jeered and accused of being a 'bad woman or even a prostitute' given the conservative attitudes in society. So a woman who did not conform was an automatic outsider, but one who sought to work for her fellow workers was, by definition, the ultimate outsider.

Nazma has always been unusual: fearless and with great self-belief and confidence that belied her poor, working-class background, especially in a society that has a very rigid class structure.

Nazma started work with her mother in a garment factory and almost immediately became involved in fighting to improve conditions. Her father urged her to toe the line and keep her head down or she would lose her job. She ignored him and was fired for her relentless dedication in fighting for her rights and those of her fellow workers.

Indeed, to understand how difficult it is to fight for workers' rights in Bangladesh, it is important to understand the social distance between the sweat-shop workers and the employers and managers. The latter perceive the workers as so far below them that the idea of any kind of contact outside the workplace is utterly inconceivable. Nazma's confidence in being able to take on the employers when they are so hostile under almost every heading is all the more remarkable.

Her members have an unshakable trust in Nazma. Her courage was highlighted again recently in a major dispute with Beximco, one of the country's leading industrial conglomerates, when several workers were fired without benefits or compensation. A tense situation prevailed outside one of their factories when Nazma arrived and struggled through the crowds to negotiate with the police who were trying to break up the strike. She was arrested and hustled into a police vehicle and taken away. Although subsequently released and the dispute settled, it gives a good illustration of the 'rough house' nature of industrial relations in the country as employers remain, sometimes violently, resistant to the very idea of workers forming trade unions to improve their often less than subsistence conditions.

In fact, as Nazma also emphasised, it is not just the very low wages, they also have to work to improve the dangerous working conditions and practices that have resulted in the deaths of several hundred women and young girls in factory fires over the years. Sexual harassment and physical violence in the workplace are also common and I witnessed first hand during a factory visit a shop-floor supervisor physically abusing a worker.

Fire drills are unheard of and a common practice is to lock workers into the factories, especially when rush orders must be met, which can sometimes mean spending the night on the premises.

One of the most serious tragedies in recent years took place at the Chowdery Knitwear factory in Narshindhi outside the capital, Dhaka, where fifty-one workers were burnt to death, locked in with no chance of escape when a fire started. Many of the charred remains of the workers, some as young as ten years old, were found at the metal window grills where they died as they struggled to get out.

That story only made about a paragraph in *The Irish Times* and got virtually no publicity in other newspapers in this part of the world. The low news value placed on the lives of these hard-working Bangladeshis inspired us to go to Bangladesh to film the documentary *Race to the Bottom*. Nazma, on camera, revealed in compelling terms the injustice and unfairness her members must endure, being forced to risk their lives for a few cents an hour, in a country where women have no other employment opportunities.

But the remarkable thing is how we have, through

ignorance, turned not only Nazma but all sweat-shop workers into outsiders. They are invisible. One of the great ironies is that many courageous women in this part of the world probably work hard every day defending and advancing the rights of those who are exploited and abused while wearing clothes produced by the sweat-shop workers all across the so-called Third World.

But many in the fashion industry are aware of this scandal and work hard to avoid it being exposed. While doing a radio interview about *Race to the Bottom* recently, the producer informed me as I was leaving the studio that his wife worked for a leading department store and they were very worried about the brutal exploitation being exposed in the sweat shops.

For me this is a classic example of how we create outsiders. We do not ask questions, even when we suspect something is wrong. The great scandal at the heart of the global garment industry is not a new story. Our documentary is probably one of many that has been made about it. But the fact that the brutal exploitation goes on relentlessly, and the big department stores and international brands are allowed to hide behind bogus codes of conduct that are not enforced, only serves to underline why we have outsiders.

The women and young girls who make up the majority of the workers in the Bangladesh garment industry want to keep their jobs. They do not want consumer boycotts as they told me, they want fair wages and decent conditions. The fact that this industry has transformed one of the poorest countries in Asia from being an aid-dependent to a trade-dependent economy over the last number of years, while they are worse off today than they were ten years ago, underlines the fact that we cannot tackle poverty without addressing the brutal conditions in the sweat shops.

Women in conservative Bangladesh have traditionally been outsiders in their society. However, one of the great paradoxes at the heart of the garment industry, which explains why the women are so desperate to keep their jobs, is that being able to earn money independently, even very meagre wages, has given them a measure of independence and liberation.

They know they are exploited. Many are well aware of the risks they expose themselves to working in the garment factories. But there are no alternative employment opportunities.

In global terms, the garment workers are outsiders. Nazma Aktor and her fellow trade unionists are trying to change that. For now, our ignorance is keeping them outside.

Anne Daly

AN OUTSIDER ON THE INSIDE TRACK

SÉAMUS DOOLEY

Dick Walsh may seem a strange choice for inclusion in an anthology about outsiders. He had a distinguished career as a jounalist and, on his retirement in October 2002, had served as Political Editor and subsequently as Assistant Editor of *The Irish Times*.

One month before his death, in the cosy surroundings of Buswells' Hotel, in the shadow of Leinster House, Dick Walsh made his last public appearance among the political elite of Irish society. An Taoiseach Bertie Ahern led the attendance at the reception in Dick's honour, which also included former Taoiseach Garret FitzGerald and an impressive collection of former cabinet ministers, serving and retired public representatives and a large number of journalistic and trade-union colleagues.

The manner in which political correspondents are required to operate leads to a dangerous closeness between politicians and members of the press gallery. In Leinster House and the House of Commons, reporters face the challenge of maintaining a professional distance from those with whom they live and work on an hourly basis.

Most rise to the challenge, but others go native, becoming embroiled in the personalities and the mechanics of the Oireachtas rather than interpreting the social and economic implications of the vast sea of documentation that floods their offices in Kildare Street.

Dick Walsh never became a political insider. There was nothing cosy or comfortable about him and he was always careful of spin doctors bearing gifts in the shape of dubious leaks. He was always suspicious of what he once termed 'the sly and mighty'.

Dick enjoyed a privileged position in Irish journalism, shaping and influencing editorial policy in *The Irish Times*. He was provided with a weekly pulpit to expound his views and, from there, he challenged the establishment, raging with elegant ferocity against those who viewed the world only through the prism of the markets.

As the obituary in *The Irish Times*, following his death on 11th March 2003, noted, his was a voice 'which would tremble with Swiftian savage indignation when it targeted the follies, corruption and hypocrisy of modern Irish life and especially politics'.

Dick was greatly honoured when Alice Leahy invited both of us to contribute to this anthology. We spoke about the project and the work of Trust. While working in London as a young journalist, Dick found himself, for a short time, homeless and, throughout his career, was a champion of social justice.

No doubt Dick would have used the opportunity to reflect on our failure to use our new-found wealth to improve the lot of the poor.

In one of his last columns before his retirement, he was strongly critical of the Church establishment, but praised campaigners, such as Sean Healy, Gordon Linney and Sr Stanislaus Kennedy, whom he declared 'annoy the hell out of the Thatcherites and send some of the bishops into paroxysms of rage and resentment'.

He went on: 'They know that those who pay for the secrecy and the silences, the evasions and the corner-cutting are the very people who might have benefited from reform when this was the richest State in Europe – but didn't – and will pay again when the bad days return.'

Dick had a unique understanding of Irish society and

a trawl through the archives of *The Irish Times* is at once uplifting and depressing. Uplifting because of the clarity and passion behind the headlines, depressing because one realises that a prophetic voice has been forever silenced.

He wrote with rare compassion and understanding. On the death of Brendan O'Donnell, he wrote a moving column on the lessons to be learned about the failure of society to heed the signals of O'Donnell's disturbed childhood behaviour. And as he always did, Dick was looking for answers rather than simply attributing blame.

As a political pundit, he had a rare insight into political culture. He was often scorned by politicians, and by Fianna Fáilers in particular, as being biased and unfair. Dick was certainly not an objective commentator, but he did not operate to a hidden agenda – he wore his left-wing heart on his sleeve.

He was always upfront and never left the reader in any doubt as to where he stood. He was the friend of the underdog and used his voice on behalf of those who had none, or those whose voices were ignored.

The product of a relatively well-off Clare family, he was born in Cratloe, on 29th October 1937, the eldest of a family of two sons and two daughters. His father, Sean, and his father before him, had been the principal teachers in the local National School. He belonged to a rural radical tradition in the spirit of Peadar O'Donnell and James Gralton of Leitrim – a list to which the names of his friend Jack McQuillan and Noël Browne can be added.

In writing about politics, Dick's analysis was informed by his background. He grew up in a family and community where, as he wrote himself, it was believed to be 'faintly heretical' to criticise de Valera.

As a political commentator, Dick enjoyed the friendship of politicians from a wide spectrum, but he had a particular affection for Jack Lynch, a conservative politician who would not have shared Walsh's radical vision. Their friendship owed much to a mutual love of Munster hurling, but Dick also admired Lynch's commitment to constitutional politics. While he was critical of gombeenism, Dick Walsh was a strong defender of politics and despised cynical hurlers on the ditch.

He started his journalistic career in *The Clare Champion* in the late 1950s, at a time when journalism was certainly not well paid or seen as a respectable profession. At this time, he also joined the NUJ, and began a lifelong association with the trade-union movement. Dick was a wonderful storyteller and many of his tales related to his early days cycling to meetings and matches among his beloved highways and byways of Clare.

He combined local journalism with writing poetry and, in 1958, *The Clare Champion* published his slim volume entitled *New Rain on the Leaves.*

From Clare, he moved to the *Irish Press* in Dublin where he met Ruth Kelly, who was Woman's Editor and who he married on Valentine's Day in 1960. During this time, he recalled attending meetings of a left-wing Catholic movement, which identified social justice as part of the Church mission long before the term 'liberation theology' had been coined. By the time that phrase had become vogue, Dick had abandoned religion but never lost his respect for radical churchmen and women.

After their marriage, Dick and Ruth moved to London where he worked for several local newspapers and where their daughters, Francesca and Suzanne, were born. He was actively involved in defending the rights of Irish building workers and helped edit a bulletin for them. That experience forged much of his later thinking.

He returned to Ireland in the early 1960s, working in Dublin and later on the *Connacht Tribune* in Galway. He worked in the *Irish Press* again and, eventually, found his journalistic home in *The Irish Times*, working initially as a sub-editor and then as a general reporter.

At the outbreak of the Troubles, he covered some of the most turbulent days in the history of Northern Ireland, witnessing the burning of Catholic homes off the Falls Road and the arrival of the British army in August 1969. He has been credited with using his influence in the left-wing circles in which he moved at the time to urge the official Republican movement to abandon violence in favour of direct politics.

In later years, he was a passionate supporter of the Good Friday Agreement and a trenchant critic of Sinn Féin. One memorable phrase stands out when, during an impasse in those talks, he warned that no ship should be sunk 'for want of a lick of green paint'.

After his time in the North, Dick was posted to Dublin, joining NUJ veteran and esteemed political correspondent Michael McInerney at a time when coverage of politics was decidedly differential.

His relationship with Jack Lynch stood him in good stead – some critics felt he was too close to him, and to a distant cousin, Des O'Malley, although he became a strong critic of the economic policies of the Progressive Democrats.

On the other hand, he had a deep suspicion of Charles J Haughey that, in time, grew into an obsessive loathing. The feeling was more or less mutual. On one occasion at a press conference, Haughey chided Walsh for not referring to him as 'Taoiseach' exclaiming, 'Everyone else addresses me as Taoiseach, you call me Mr Haughey, have you no respect for the position of Taoiseach?'

Dick sardonically retorted, 'It is precisely because I have respect for the position of Taoiseach...'

In the 1980s, Dick Walsh wrote a personal account of Fianna Fáil called *The Party: Inside Fianna Fáil*. In it, he summed up his view of Haughey, describing him as dominating Fianna Fáil 'in a way that no other leader had done, in the style of an east-European head of state whose basilisk stare follows his citizens wherever they go'.

The connection between Haughey and big business was one of Dick's obsessions and even his closest friends sometimes felt he was going too far. But on his retirement, Dick could smile wryly as we commented, in a strange but apt mixed metaphor, that 'his hobby horses had come home to roost'.

He took no pleasure in the fact that tribunals had proved him right, just as the crisis in *The Irish Times* had vindicated his long-held belief that the Trust that controlled the newspaper should be reformed. Unusually for a journalist, Dick seldom said, 'I told you so.'

For much of his life, Dick struggled with health problems. He was diagnosed as having spondylitis, causing curvature of the spine. He was in constant pain but never complained. His sparkling eyes never dimmed and he laughed off a series of brushes with death with such ease that his final passing was all the harder to take.

Dick often filed copy from his hospital bed and, in recent years, worked from home, using the phone to keep in touch with a wide circle of friends. For a man who loved company, it was a terrible burden, but it made his trips to Dublin all the more special.

During the financial crisis at *The Irish Times* in 2001 and 2002, he was a constant support to his NUJ colleagues. During that period, he was hospitalised and, not for the first time, we thought we had lost him. 'I heard them saying, "This is a lucky man, he died last night and should still be dead,'" he told me. Adding hastily, 'How are the negotiations going?'

On another occasion, Dick was invited to attend an NUJ conference in Ennis. On arrival, we learned he had travelled, complete with mobile oxygen unit, by train to Limerick and had then taken an Expressway bus to Ennis. He exchanged banter about Clare hurling with the driver, who changed route to let Dick off at the door of the West County Hotel.

That night Dick stayed up too late, chatting and listening to songs, eventually running out of oxygen. An emergency supply was needed and so he phoned his brother Johnny, another journalist, who agreed to make the cross-country journey without complaint. It was typical of the spirit of both men.

Dick took his illness for granted. It informed his thinking on social issues – he knew all about the inadequacies of the health service and had a strong admiration for hospital staff, but he never really regarded himself as disabled. The disability was one more challenge to be faced.

He used his talents with style, elegance and humour. Above all else, he hated the selfish vulgarity of the new Ireland. As his friend John McGahern recalled at Dick's funeral service, his disdain would be summed up in cutting phrases such as, 'Love-ly peop-le… Plen-ty of mon-ey… *No* man-ners.'

Dick was not a Christian, but his understanding and compassion and his commitment to ethical standards was certainly close to Christianity.

As he wrote in 1998, in his *Irish Times* Saturday column:

> Ireland in the 1990s has made some headway on sex: it still fumbles nervously with class. The joke in the play [*No Sex Please – We're British*] was that

sex lay, if you'll forgive the phrase, at the bottom of all things British in the late 1960s and early 1970s.

The irony here is that class has been at the heart and head of all things Irish for a lot longer, yet we still approach it crab-like, under cover. Class is, as sex was, a subject best avoided in polite company.

Dick Walsh remained to the end an outsider, always willing to raise issues which polite company would prefer to ignore.

Séamus Dooley

AN ENCOUNTER

TIM DOYLE

Nuala is a student garda based in Dublin. Her role as a guardian of society was starkly illustrated when she encountered her first prisoner:

I was thrilled – a dream come true – being a police-woman in a busy station in my own city. Teeming with incidents, experiences and prisoners. I would break all records. First duty – night patrol – 10pm–6am. The sergeant details the car crew to 'show me our patch'. It's the back seat of the patrol car for yours truly.

10.05pm. First call. 'Car being broken into at…Culprit fleeing in the direction of…'

10.10pm. The patrol car skids to a halt in a lane way. Suspect being held. Angry, dirty and dishevelled and with downcast eyes, he grudgingly gives me his name. Something about him? His eyes flash into mine. My God! It was Damien; a young man who had been born and reared a few doors from my home and who I had babysat up to a few years previously. Resignation melted his antagonism as he offered his correct name and address.

En route to the station, he sat beside me. I kept visualising him as a child – his innocence – his respect for his parents, his reliance and obedience to my every wish. I began to experience difficulty dealing with the emotional impact of the altercation. He began to sob. I wanted to take him in my arms and give him a cuddle. In the station, he wouldn't leave my side. He told me he had been 'on the streets' for a while. I couldn't rid myself of the babysitting memories. Being summoned to deal with another task was a relief. On my return, Damien had been charged and bailed.

The next morning, after my duties ended, I passed

his home. I felt a sense of shame as if I had failed him and his family. I couldn't reconcile the past with the present and experienced a great sadness that memories of the fondest kind had been uprooted overnight. I wanted to call and tell his mom but I was torn between being a concerned neighbour and my responsibility as a guardian of the peace to the wider community. Even though I was physically tired, sleep was a stupor and I realised how my first garda experience had turned my private world upside down. In truth, I was fearful of the consequences.

The following day, Damien failed to appear in court. My anxieties, which were still spiralling out of control, settled into a feeling of helplessness. I began to question my career. Is my job going to be arresting people and not caring for them? I questioned my resolve. Was I too softhearted to be a garda?

Relief came in the form of another period of garda training that took me down the country. Being away from the predicament gave me some respite and, on my return, I resolved to persevere with my career.

After the training phase, I returned to my station. One evening, I was on beat duty in a city street when I caught sight of Damien. He was wandering aimlessly, holding a partly chewed Styrofoam cup containing a few coins. Even though admitting he was still 'on the streets', he seemed happy to see me. I warned him of the dangers of sleeping rough. He said he'd be all right that his family didn't matter any more. I got annoyed and told him he was responsible for his own actions and that he couldn't blame anyone but himself for his lifestyle. He bristled with agitation but remained silent.

I felt my reference to his home had hit a nerve, as from then the conversation was open, honest and centred on his previous existence. I was so delighted with our encounter that I told him to contact me in my station if I could be of assistance. It wasn't long before my offer backfired. Within a few days some of my colleagues at the station were asking if I'd babysat Damien.

I discovered that he had been dropping my name when arrested for begging. To some colleagues I became known as 'Nuala the babysitter from hell'. That was hurtful, but I remained committed and was determined to have another heart-to-heart with Damien.

At the start of my next duty, I headed for his patch. He occupied his usual street corner complete with cardboard seat; head slumped onto his chest and one outstretched arm clutching his container. I was disgusted and beckoned him upright. I told him I didn't like him using my name to help get him out of trouble. He countered that he didn't like the way people knew about his background and accused me of ratting on him. I told him things like that worked both ways but my main concern was to get him off the streets and back home. I noted a flicker of interest and lashed into a mutual anecdote from our babysitting days. His grimy face cracked up. We talked and I kept the conversation centred on his home. Suddenly, he blurted that he wasn't wanted there. I responded that it wasn't him but his lifestyle that wasn't welcome.

The following day when I arrived for work, a colleague approached me and said he had arrested Damien for begging but he was willing to ignore the offence if I had a word with him. His approach gave me affirmation that a humane intervention was more potent than conventional methods of dealing with public order offences. Damien was slumped in a cell, but he stood respectfully as I entered. I never mentioned the surroundings or the details of his incarceration, but launched into the latest update from the home front. I told him I had seen his mom earlier in the day and that she looked great. Also I had spotted his brother driving the family car and, finally, I put before him the image of his sister, a beautiful child who was turning into a lovely teenager.

After that, he began to shy away from me in public but I waylaid him at every turn and kept reminding him of his home and family. Suddenly, he disappeared. Days moved into a week without a sighting. I canvassed my colleagues to no avail. I was so concerned that I was on the point of reporting him missing when he reappeared. I'll never forget the day, time or place. It was my station and I was on the late shift. As I entered, an impeccably dressed young man approached me. It was Damien, looking so well I hardly recognised him. He told me he had 'gone offside' to get his head right. He said he was going home. We had the best cuddle ever. As we parted he said, 'See you'se around.'

'Yes,' I countered, 'only around our homes from now on.'

His reply was unforgettable. 'Jaysus, with you around here you'd swear I never left the place. You never gave up babysitting me.'

Tim Doyle

SPIKE MILLIGAN:
THE OUTSIDE GOON

DANNY ERSKINE

When I was asked to write a piece about an outsider who had done good things, one of the first people I thought of was Spike Milligan, a man I knew little of but was interested to learn more about.

Through my research, I found a remarkable man: a soldier, a poet, a writer, an actor, a musician, a patient and a comedian. A man who suffered with bipolar disorder (the medical term for manic depression) and yet was voted the funniest person of the last 1,000 years in a BBC poll in 1999. A man who could bring light into thousands of peoples lives... but not his own.

Below is a poem written by Spike during his time in hospital between 1953 and 1954:

Manic Depression
The pain is too much
A thousand grim winters
grow in my head,
in my ears
the sound of the
coming dead.
All seasons
All sane
All living
All pain.
No opiate to lock still
my sense.
Only left,
the body locked tenses.

Spike once wrote in a letter: 'The world is a bloody awful place – it always will be and, as long as you approach it with that in mind, you don't get so many disappointments.' He then proceeded to end the letter 'Love, Light and Peace'.

This goes to show what a confusing illness bipolar disorder is.

He was born Terence Alan Milligan in Ahmed Nagar, India, to an Irish-born officer in the British army, in April 1918. Although he lived most of his life in England and served in the Royal Artillery in Italy and North Africa during World War II, he was declared stateless in 1960 and took Irish citizenship.

He campaigned on environmental issues, particularly unnecessary noise (which was a problem for him mainly due to the shellshock he suffered during the war which left him more sensitive to noise than others) and animal cruelty (which saw him, in 1976, protesting beside a headstone that read 'RIP 1976–7 15,554 Antarctic Great Whales Sentenced To Death By Man's Greed' outside the Japanese embassy on the first day of the whaling season). Later, in 1986, he attempted to feed 28lbs of cooked pasta to the manager of Harrod's Food Hall nearly equalling the 6lbs of maize force fed to geese to enlarge their livers to make pâté de foie gras.

He not only protested for animals but also for humans. In 1972, a young woman was sent to prison for abducting a baby, she did this out of love, and Spike felt for her as she was being treated as a criminal rather than just a confused woman. Spike did not believe that she was innocent but wanted her to have a homely atmosphere 'with lots of love', so he decided to write to her. When he did not receive a reply, he persisted until he did. He also wrote to the governor of the prison to ensure that she received her mail. I really admire him for these things. He spoke out for animals because they have no voice of their own and helped this young woman when most others simply condemned her.

During the war, Spike's twenty-five pound gun jumped due to recoil and rolled down a hill, narrowly missing another gun unit. He went after it and, asking whether anyone had seen a gun, one man replied, 'What colour?' His name was Harry Secombe. Spike met Harry one more time during the war while working as a comedian in the combined services entertainment unit; they would become best friends till Secombe's death. Even then, Spike showed his odd sense of humour by saying, 'I'm glad he died before me, because I didn't want him to sing at my funeral.' But Secombe had the last laugh as a recording of him singing was played at Spike's memorial service.

After the war, Secombe introduced Spike to Peter Sellers and Michael Bentine. The four would go on to change comedy forever, although their friendship would endure some hardships, mainly due to Spike's illness. Sellers was once forced to lock his door against a knife-wielding Spike and, on another occasion, Secombe and Sellers had to break in to Spike's dressing room for fear that he was suicidal. Eventually, Lithium was found to be the most effective treatment for Spike.

Through most of the 1930s and 1940s, Spike played jazz trumpet and went on to play jazz guitar in The Bill Hall Trio, but he couldn't help adding in comedy sketches to the act. They performed originally for the troops at concert parties but, for a short time after the war, they performed on stage.

While entertaining the troops during the war, Spike began to write parodies of popular plays, a style of comedy that would be displayed in *The Goon Show* and would later inspire entertainers such as Monty Python. But

writing so much would take its toll on Spike, and having
to write a show a week would provoke as many as ten
mental breakdowns.

Spike's big break came when Jimmy Grafton, a some-
time comedy writer for the BBC, persuaded executives
at the BBC to let Milligan, Sellers, Secombe and Bentine
go on air as *Those Crazy People* (the name was shortly
changed to *The Goon Show*, Spike's preferred name). The
show was a huge success. Its fans included Prince Charles
who was to become a close friend. In 1994, when Spike
received the British comedy lifetime achievement award,
a telegram of congratulations from Prince Charles was
read out. Spike paused and then said, 'Grovelling little
bastard.' It was a classic Spike moment and a classic Spike
reaction. He later asked, 'I suppose a knighthood is out
of the question now?' But finally, in 2000, he was
awarded an honorary knighthood (honorary due to his
Irish citizenship).

Spike's most lasting project was the *Q* series, running
from 1969 to 1982, but not everything Spike did was as
popular or successful and he provoked a good deal of
controversy in LWT's *Curry and Chips* in which he played
a Pakistani.

Spike also wrote many poems for children who meant
so much to him – he considered them to be our only
hope.

On 27th February 2002, Spike died from kidney failure aged eighty-three at his home in East Sussex.

I chose Spike Milligan as my outsider because I believe he was an amazing man, changing comedy forever
while fighting a constant battle against the emotionally
crippling bipolar disorder that, ironically, may have been
the source of all his genius.

What I suspect is that he is now in a far happier place,
probably writing sketches, sending up God, and laugh-

ing the days away with his good friends Harry, Peter
and Michael, freed from his earthly torments.

The heart that is soonest awake to the flowers
Is always the first to be touched by the thorns
Thomas Moore (1779–1892)

Danny Erskine

PRISON BARS

In the 1980s, the Arts Council launched a project called
Writers in Prisons. The immediate joke was 'and that's
where they all deserve to be'! But beyond the humour,
there was a great appreciation of this innovative and
visionary idea: a selection of writers would be invited to
visit Irish prisons, to meet interested prisoners and to
conduct literary workshops.

I was asked to participate and, within the following
years, I spent time in Mountjoy, Arbour Hill, Wheat-
field, Portlaoise and Cork prisons. It was a project that
filled me with trepidation and, even now, years later, I
can perfectly recall the sounds and the smells of these
places and – more importantly – the appearance, the
looks and the behaviour of the men forced to live within
their walls.

The planned programme was that, each Saturday
morning, I would work with a group of selected prisoners. Ostensibly, we would explore their feelings
through their writings – but, in reality, I came to know
them best through conversations about their lives, their
plight, their sense of survival and their search for dignity in this most undignified world.

I knew then that I would never forget any of these
men – and, indeed, I haven't. But there is one man that
I remember more than all the others – simply because I
witnessed not only his despair but also his redemption.
I will call him Robert and I will also disguise both his
prison and his crime. But I can never disguise the effect
that he (and his imprisonment) had on me and my life.

Nothing prepares any of us for prison. We can read
all the books, see all the films, hear all the stories, but
when that heavy door closes behind you and you enter

the echoing world of lost souls, a heaviness runs through your body that is both despairing and terrifying.

Of course, I was lucky. Whenever I entered a prison, I knew that I would be home again within three hours. But inside, I would meet men who would not see their homes or sit on a bus or feel rain on their faces for the next three months or three years or thirteen years. Instead, they were condemned to exist in a world ruled by strange laws, where the passage of time was marked by the rattle of keys, where friendships were born of shared sorrows, where months passed without either surprise or satisfaction.

This is not to say that the prisons were anything like the fiction of Dumas or the reality of Wilde. Quite the opposite: they were bright, clean and orderly. Sometimes, they even appeared to be cheerful. Like hospitals, they tried hard to disguise the pain and unhappiness that dwelt within.

From my experience, it seemed that most prisoners made the sensible choice of simply adapting to this new world with its new hierarchy and its militaristic regulations. Day by day, they connected peripherally with the 'outside' through visits, television, reading and gossip or by simply looking up at the sky and imagining what changes are out there, beyond.

Robert was different. Of all people, he would have benefited from an integration into the system because, of all the prisoners I met, his sentence was particularly long. But he never conformed. In his quiet way, he simply refused to be part of that world. And to their credit, the authorities seemed to facilitate this independence by granting him minor privileges. So, when I arrived at his prison, he was not part of the group. When I spoke with Robert, we sat in a cell, alone.

He had few friends. While other prisoners dressed in

optimistic casual clothes, Robert wore monastic sandals, a mortuary brown suit and grew his beard long and shaggy. When others exercised and stayed fit, he would sit quietly and read, as though determined to slow everything down to his own selected pace. When I sat with him in his cell, he would talk quietly and deliberately as he either unwrapped sweets with the meticulousness of a watchmaker or painstakingly rolled his cigarettes as though he were carrying out brain surgery.

My first visit with him was fraught, strained and almost aggressive in its silence. It was as though we knew both too little and too much about each other. He would have known, of course, that I knew *why* he was there. And I knew that he was suspicious as to why *I* was there. It became impossible, in that first meeting, to break down these barriers – and so we each indulged in an offensive politeness, an exchanging of vacuous and patronising pleasantries.

But the thaw set in quickly. And soon, he was reading his poetry and his stories – usually about people who were innocently imprisoned, either mentally or physically – and, every so often, he would glance up at me, his eyes full of challenge and conviction. When the readings finished, our discussions would begin – and, whenever I confided concerns about the writing of my own plays, he would respond with small intimacies about his life.

Our relationship grew stronger and my last visit – six weeks later – was full of loud debate, joyful reminiscences and expressions of gratitude from each of us. And then, we were close to my departure time, always heralded by the jangle of keys against his cell door.

We both became quieter and the atmosphere of our initial meeting returned. Now, however – with trust in place – he suddenly spoke about himself and, for the

first time, I heard some of the cold reality that had inspired his poetry and his fiction. He admitted that, despite his aspirations, the prospects of his near-future
freedom were bleak. 'But,' he added, and there was a
sparkle of defiance in his weary eyes, 'I am always hope-
ful.'

His hopes were greater than I would have imagined
them – and I was unsure of how to wish him well. I did
it as best I could. He wished me success with my plays
and wondered if he would ever get to see one. Then it
was time for me to leave – to walk from his cell, along
the wide corridor, through the opening and closing gates
and into the sunlight, knowing that, for years to come,
his life would remain constantly monotonous within
the echoing shouts of those stone walls, the rattling
keys, the rules and regulations and, always, the tenuous,
fading hope.

In the following weeks, then months, then years, I
occasionally thought about him. As my life changed –
for better and for worse – I realised that his remained
constant. I imagined that if I suddenly visited him, all
the timetables, the sounds, the lights-on and lights-out
would be just as before.

Then, some six years later, I was at the premiere of
one of my plays. These are, for me, always times of
high anxiety and, at the play's interval, I usually busy
myself by simply trying to avoid the theatre-goers and
any soul-destroying hints of disapproval. However, on
this occasion, I had friends visiting from abroad, so I
broke all my rules and stood with them in the crowd at
the bar, awaiting the second act.

We were having a pleasant conversation – avoiding
all judgement of the play – when a hand squeezed my
arm, forcing me to turn.

The man in front of me was tall, grey-haired, dressed
in a sports blazer, white shirt and red cravat. He was

holding a small whiskey in his hand and now he extended his free hand and said, 'I hope the second act will be as good as the first.'

I thanked him for his kindness and was about to turn away, when he said, 'You don't remember me, do you?' I looked at him, totally lost, and had begun to mutter my apologies when he cut me off with one word. 'Robert,' he said.

It was his eyes that I then recognised. In the past, I had only seen them as though they were sleeping, waiting. Now they were alive and alert. The defiance had left them, now replaced with an enthusiasm. Suddenly, I was embracing him and trying to believe that this was the same man who was once dressed in mortuary brown and monastic sandals, rolling ragged cigarettes and living in a world of distant shouts, jangled keys and echoes.

Then he was introducing me to his wife, to his children, to his friends. He was offering to buy more drinks, he was joking, laughing and debating. He was normal. And then, we were being summoned to return to the theatre – not by the rattle of locks, but by the tinkling of bells.

And so he left me at the bar, merrily shouting back his good wishes for Act Two. I had never asked him how he was *out* of prison, no more than I ever asked him how he was *in* there. I have since heard the reason for his early release – but it is of no importance. No more than the details of his conviction. All that was important in that moment was to see him walk away, light-hearted, into the theatre, like a beached seal being returned to the ocean or a trapped animal being released again into the wild.

And I thought back to those grey days in his prison cell and I believe that, in there, he saw something that I could never see. Behind those tired, weary eyes, I think he always saw a sports blazer, a cravat and a glass of whiskey. It was a vision that was always there, buried deep, awaiting its release, nurtured by nothing more than hope.

I never saw him again. So I don't even know what he thought of the second act. Perhaps he wanted to meet me and tell me. Maybe he even tried, but gave up in the hustle of a First Night. More likely, he felt that there was nothing more to say. Our dialogue was finished – just like in the play – and nothing could change what had gone before. A play had been launched that night and it was now out in the world. And he too was out in the world – free and dignified at last.

Bernard Farrell

THE ROAD

TONY GILL

I come from a working-class background, but you could say that we were middle class. I had two brothers and one sister. As a young man, I joined the army but, when my parents got old, I left so that I could look after them.

When my parents died, they left everything to my brothers and sister, I was left to my own devices. I hadn't got a clue, not a bloody clue, how would I? I never had to look after myself; my parents were always there. I was just an unpaid servant, who followed orders and did what was asked of me.

I was an abused child, abused by a man in our house, and nothing was ever said. I don't hold grudges, but I can't ever forget.

As I said, I never came from a home – oh, I had food on the table, the place was immaculate. It was big, but missed one vital element: there was no love. Not even between my mother and father, not even between my brothers and sister. Now my father and mother I could understand. My father was brought up hard in the country in Longford. How can you give love when you never knew it? The early part of their marriage was rough. My mother was a hard worker, an honest worker, and she did care, but she never put her arms around you. If I wanted a dinky car she would buy me it, and my dad would give me my picture money, but I didn't want that. My father died of cancer.

The day I was turned out onto the streets, I had a bag, a dog and just £2 of my own. I started to walk the streets, and soon drank to ease the pain. The people who saw me on the streets helped me in many ways. The street became my escape from responsibility, my escape from reality. Any responsibilities I had, had all

gone. I felt at ease with myself. People say you can forgive, but you never ever, ever forget – and I don't forget
the abuse that happened to me from the age of six. Perhaps that was the main reason that I started to drink,
but then we can all give those stupid reasons.

When I ended up on the streets, I became a quick
learner. The first thing I learnt was to stay out of trouble – don't get yourself into situations that you might
regret later. I learnt that I had to look after myself, provide for myself, and that is what I do. You see I have a
knack – the right approach. I won't ask people for the
price of a loaf if I actually want a drink. I tell the truth.
If I need a drink, I ask for money for a drink. Most of
the time, I get what I need. I also learnt that life on the
streets is cold and tough. When you see gangs of people drinking together, they're not friends. All they are
doing is sharing their loneliness and misery, and the only
escape for them is alcohol or worse. I've never taken
drugs or gone down that line, but I can understand it. I
don't approve of it, yet I can understand it.

I have slept in doorways, I have slept in train stations, I have even slept in police stations – not because
of being arrested, but just because it was somewhere to
come in out of the cold. I have attempted suicide once;
my attempt lasted for about ten seconds, because the
water was too cold. I didn't want to commit suicide, I
was just pissed off and had had enough. Things along
the way are hard for a lot of people and even more so
for people who have nowhere to live. A drink will more
often than not get you by. People who are on narcotics
don't stand a chance, they become rude and vulgar, even
towards the drunks on the streets. I can't really say that
they become dirty because I've soiled myself at times.
Life on the streets can be that difficult.

These people here at Trust, Alice and Gerry, they
got me sober – no psychiatrists, no doctors, Pat in Trust

is my doctor. Pat's the best psychiatrist I have. As for Alice, I love her. Not because she treats me any more special than anyone else, but because she treats me as me. I know if I was in trouble, within reason, she would help me. I am no longer alone, but people tell me you are always on your own. Being on your own and being lonely are two different ball games. I do like my own company, but there are times when I can build a wall against reality. It gets higher and higher and thicker and thicker, and at the end you end up with a mental breakdown.

I was halfway through a wall like this when I met a guy. He wasn't the most intelligent, but he was a nice bloke. We drank together, we never fought, we never stole from each other – there was no need to. We both worked the streets. I did Westland Row, where I'm well known, he'd do his own place. During the day, we'd meet up. He never asked what you had in your pocket, nor I him, but we would say, 'How are the accounts today?' and we'd start emptying our pockets, and we'd find we'd made good money. We'd both have different people we'd tap and different ways of doing it. The street is the greatest university in life provided you want to learn.

I'm thankful to those brilliant women on the soup run. I can't abide soup, but they used to bring me down cake and horrible cheese sandwiches. I hate cheese sandwiches, but I wouldn't throw them away. I'd eat them even though I didn't like them, because someone came out of their way to bring them down. Someone out there cares.

We are not an island. We can make ourselves an island, and I've been doing that for years, but now I've found a rowboat. Where the goddamn thing is I don't know.

I have a friend who owns an art gallery. I sat outside his place for thirteen years begging. If I was to ask him for money, I would normally get it. I'd do a little bit of cleaning here and a little something there, and he trusts me. He even let me sleep inside the gallery. He knew that nothing would go missing. Any money left there overnight would still be there in the morning. I might take a bottle of wine or two, but I'd always tell him in the morning, and he'd tell me to settle up on Thursday, which meant it would never ever happen.

A lot of people say that rich people don't care, they're wrong. The working class can be the worst. They put us down. I've been called more names by them, and names do hurt. I have a good sense of humour, and I'm sharp. If I want to take somebody apart, I do, but now I don't bother unless they get to me. As I said before, I don't want to get involved in drugs – I'm dopey enough. Who would want to go round dopier? These hands were made for creativity, not stealing. Believe it or not, some people do give comfort to us. A woman getting off the Dart, running because she's late for work, who shouts 'morning!' is worth a fortune – even more than a ₹20 note, because she sees you.

I recently spent some time in hospital – I got clots in the legs – in fact I'm going to lose my big toe soon, but the doctors are happy, they know what they're doing, so I'm not worried. I was in hospital for three weeks – it was only supposed to be a week, but this Nigerian doctor knew I was on the streets and kept me in for three.

A community welfare officer got me a room. It's a big room that's got central heating, a fridge and a double bed. I keep it immaculately clean, you see once you've been in the dirt and you have the chance to get out of it, you take it.

I'm happy there, but I found it difficult at times to live to the rules and regulations. I often used to play my radio till six or seven in the morning because I couldn't sleep. It was probably because I had spent nineteen years on the streets. I didn't have a shower, I didn't have a bed, and I slept on the floor. Because it was here, it was in me head. Then I sat down one day and I said, 'I'm gonna be homeless.' I have no money I couldn't give a hoot. I've ¿20 in my pocket.

Happiness is a state of mind. I'm content. I hold no grudges against my parents. I hold no grudges against anybody, even those who insult me. What's the point of hating somebody? And I mean really hating. Hate is like a cancer, it grows and it kills you. But the person you hate couldn't give a hoot.

The last thing I've learnt is to live and try and understand, to be allowed to do my own thing within reason and just live and maybe this dream of being happy will come.

I miss my mate, but put the two of us together and you've got a disaster. He's married with children and all that.

All my life I've been put down, I'm not a fighter even though I was in the army.

I want to be a writer. I want to be a poet. I want to be me and just have a little place. I don't want millions, I don't want fame, I don't want fortune. I just want to get a few bob to live on to buy the things I want. What I want at the moment now I have, I have everything I want. The point is I have found something. Now I don't know how long I am going to be kept at this establishment. I have a funny feeling that I might be kept long.

Tony Gill

Which Way Are You Going Brother?

Which way are you going, brother?
Where you lead, I will follow,
When you sleep, I'll stay awake.
When you cry, I see your tears
In the night, I will wipe them away.
But where you lead, I will follow.
In your shadow I will be.
In your shadow I will walk,
Cause in your shadow I want to be.
You open the door and set me free
From the loneliness.
Fight we may, but friends we will be.
Brother, you are the same as me.

Tony Gill
21st July 2000

THE KILEELY
COMMUNITY PROJECT

ANN HIGGINS

The first part of this piece refers to a group of women with whom I have been privileged to work for the past eighteen years. They have inspired me, challenged me and loved me so that my life has been enriched. They have given their time freely to their community to nurture and enhance the quality of life of children and adults. I have spent many years of my life working with children in different capacities, as a primary school teacher, youth worker, after-school tutor and literacy tutor. I have worked in many parts of Limerick city and have been challenged to work creatively to meet the diverse needs of children and young people I have worked with. The poem at the end of this article refers to a particular day while working with a group of children when a particular incident occurred that opened my eyes and my heart to the complexities of supporting children through the sometimes dangerous path of childhood.

In the mid 1980s, I was involved in setting up the Kileely Community Project on the north side of Limerick city. It was a grass-roots project, a holistic response to learning needs within the area. When this project began, it was totally unfunded – we did not even have chairs and tables. All we had was the converted cloakroom of a small primary school, the goodwill of the staff and principal of the school and the irrepressible energy and commitment of a group of local women who undertook to nurture and develop this initiative. Although Limerick City VEC came to our aid by providing teachers for our adult-education classes, the real success of this initiative rests on the shoulders of the

local women who work on a voluntary basis to provide
opportunities for learning for their neighbours and provide a warm and welcoming environment where women
and men and children have opportunities to be part of
a nurturing learning community.

Consider a small community that forms part of the
wedge of corporation housing on the north side of Limerick city: a community with over 16 per cent unemployment in the mid-1980s; without a tradition of adult
or continuing education; without a community centre,
sports hall or playing pitch; and where, according to the
1986 census, 53.2 per cent of the population had left
school by fifteen.

Now consider a group of courageous local women
who chose to stand and work together against that back-
drop to bring changes and facilities to their community.
Consider women who had families to rear, dinners to
cook and who themselves had left school at an early
age.

These are the women who have worked on a voluntary basis with me since the mid-1980s. These women
gave, and still give, their free time to enable their community to have learning opportunities it did not have
previously.

Ita, Marie, Annette, Bernie, Annie, Bridie, Mary and
Rita were women with vision. They chose to be involved
in learning in a way unheard of previously within their
community. They recruited their neighbours, they voted
with their feet. They made a statement within their community that learning opportunities could be claimed and
made available within it.

In the early days of Kileely Community Project,
which was set up in St Lelia's Primary School, this band
of women came together to identify the learning needs
of the adult population within their community and to
celebrate their community.

Community-based adult education classes, which are

now quite widespread, were almost unheard of back then. The learning culture of the time did not include adults from within our type of community. Yet these women moved beyond the culture of the time and worked actively on a voluntary basis to develop learning opportunities within their area. The only public building was the local primary school, and it is also remarkable that Clare Finn, the principal at the time, embraced the opportunity to develop a very basic school building into a learning centre. The project could not continue to thrive and develop without the support and encouragement of the present principal, Chris Deely, and the school staff.

The women celebrated the wonderful solidarity and fun they were having. They organised dinner dances, which were held in a cleared out classroom of the school using table cloths, chairs, cutlery, plates, glasses borrowed from their homes for the night. Later, records were played and they danced and laughed and celebrated their involvement in the project.

These women probably won't make the pages of history. They continue to work quietly encouraging their neighbours to come along and be part of a learning process and part of a movement that highlights positive aspects of the community.

Ita makes sure we have a dinner dance each year and organises venue, band and food; Annette collects money on a weekly basis so that we can have an annual women's holiday or a night out in a nice restaurant; Marie, who also works as supervisor in the FÁS scheme, makes sure that we have crèche facilities to enable young mothers to attend the morning adult-education classes; Bernie, along with all the other members, brings her knowledge of community to the committee meetings to make sure that any decisions we make reflect the needs of the women involved; Annie, a gifted crafts woman, taught knitting classes for many years in the project. Bridie and

Annette and Rita worked for many years with an after-school programme.

It is very difficult to truly describe the courage and commitment of these women. They chose to be part of a process of addressing their own learning and social needs and the learning and social needs of their community. That meant they had to stand outside the community and become leaders and break new ground.

The adult classes that have run over the years have been educational and social in nature. Sometimes women come and learn new skills and develop the confidence to move up the educational ladder. Sometimes they come to enjoy being part of the heartbeat of the community where troubles are shared and confidences exchanged. Even in sometimes difficult circumstances, the family of Kileely Community Project support each other.

It is also difficult to describe the conditions that existed when the project was being set up. They sat on top of old wooden desks, boiled pots of water to provide hairdressing classes, placed a square of red carpet in the corner of a room and called it a crèche. These women organised, and still organise, daytrips, weekend holidays, dances, charity walks, summer walks, jumble sales and guest speakers – and have recently embraced asylum-seekers.

In summary, these women are my heroines, they stood up within their community. They were not paid professionals but women who reared families, cooked dinners and who have worked together for the past eighteen years to provide their community with learning opportunities and enrich the lives of adults and children alike.

These women have enriched my life beyond measure. Thank you Ita, Marie, Annette Bernie, Bridie, Mary, Annie and Rita for making my life more fulfilled by your courage and commitment and most of all by your friendship and laughter.

Child

He sits on my shoulder
Sometimes he whispers in my ear
It opens my heart like a battleaxe.

He began as a specific child
In a specific place at a specific time.

In a frozen moment our eyes met across eternity
I read the pain in his eyes
It echoed across a landscape of humiliation and fear.

He was seven years old
Condemned beyond reprieve
In a frozen moment, a frozen life chilled my bones.

Now many years later
He haunts me
Only when I am lucky
And my heart leaps with fear that I will not answer his
    call.

Now he is not a specific child, gender or colour
He is one of many children of today's Ireland
Disinherited by accident of birth.

He goes to school late without a lunch
She leaves school without a destination.

You do not know this child who broke my heart
But if you open your eyes you will see his watchful
    brother standing by the bridge
His sister takes care of younger children, herself a child.

Allow yourself to be vulnerable, to feel the pain
So your life can be disturbed by his silent cry.

Ann Higgins

OUTSIDE THE MAINSTREAM

CON HOULIHAN

A time comes in the life of every mariner when he longs for a shore job. If he gets his wish, he doesn't enjoy unalloyed happiness ever after. In this context, a friend of mine tells a little story.

He had been a ship's captain and had settled well enough into a shore job. Then, one night while travelling between Cork and Fishguard, he chanced to see his old ship. It was the loneliest moment of his life; never did he feel himself so much an outsider. Of course it was only a fleeting experience; life went on – he wasn't really an outsider at all.

Albert Camus was arguably the most fashionable writer of the post-war generation and his *The Outsider* was deemed essential reading. Its hero or, if you like, its anti-hero, isn't an outsider at all. When we first meet him, he is a young man enthralled to existentialism – at least he imagines that he is. He pretends to be free from all human emotion; he is not so much outside life as above it.

You will find real outsiders in an almost-forgotten book, *The Diary of Humphrey O'Sullivan*. He was a native of Kerry who taught school in Callan in South Kilkenny in the first half of the nineteenth century. By then, the Act of Union had caused great changes. Dublin was no longer a capital city and many of the aristocracy had moved to London. The absentee landlords were replaced by agents, a class worse than their masters. Evictions became common. O'Sullivan records the reality.

One day while out walking, he met a woman who had just been forced out of her home. She was living in the open near what had been her house. She wept bitterly and was not grateful to the new occupant of her home. 'It is I who planted those potatoes but it is he who will dig them.' She went on, 'My table and my cooking pot are in the bushes. My spinning wheel is in the ditch.' In the cruellest sense of the word, a real outsider.

In this context, I can never forget an occasion when I saw several men who were truly outsiders. It was a time when the Aer Lingus pilots had downed their wings. I had to go to the Cup Final in Wembley by boat. The train from Holyhead arrived in Paddington about four o'clock in the morning – you could call it a non-human hour. On the floors inside the great station was a scene that might have come from Dante's *Inferno*. Men of all ages, wrapped in swathes of newspaper, lay sleeping or trying to sleep. Some were talking loudly to nobody in particular. Some were experiencing nightmares. In the midst of all this misery, a little brown-faced man from the Indian sub-continent was trying to keep the place tidy, and all the while he was singing quietly to himself. Of course I didn't understand the words, but I sensed that he was singing about the skies and the fields, the hills and the streams that he might never see again.

He too was an outsider, but in a different sense. He was an exile, but the Indians and the Pakistanis in London have intimate communities. In Winmark Underground in Sydney, I also saw men sleeping on the floor in a station. There was a difference: most were Aborigines, outsiders in their own land.

I have never much liked *Ulysses* – at least to me it has too much head and too little heart. I believe, however, that if Joyce's reputation depended only on *Dubliners*, he would live. A lot of those people within its covers are outsiders, none more so than Lenehan in 'Two Gallants'. He is one of two young men who are living on their wits. While his friend, kind of, goes off to meet a girl from whom he expects to get some money, Lenehan passes the time wandering around Dublin. Eventually, hunger attacks him: he hasn't eaten since breakfast except for some biscuits he had asked two surly curates to bring him. He goes into a modest restaurant in Rutland Square. Over a plate of hot peas and a bottle of ginger beer, he looks back over his life. He realised he was tired of knocking about, pulling the devil by the tail, of shifts and intrigues. He would be thirty-one in November. Would he never get a good job? Would he never have a home of his own? He thought how pleasant it would be to have a warm fire to sit down by, and a good dinner to sit down to. Lenehan to me is a more tragic figure than any in Shakespeare – he is a real person.

L S Lowry, the painter who chronicled the common life of Manchester so brilliantly, would have understood him. Or at least he would have tried: he was fascinated by those who had fallen off life's wheel. He was fascinated by the history of those people who were living on the margin. He met many of them in the course of his work as a rent collector and he used to wonder at what point the graph of their lives had turned down. Was it sudden and dramatic, or did it happen almost imperceptibly? Some people were able to tell him; others weren't sure – they had just drifted away from the mainstream of life. The same question often bothered me, especially in London. There I often met grand, decent men who seemed to have lost all interest in life. Many spent much of their time in the pubs, but drink wasn't the source of their loneliness – it was only a symptom.

Some years ago, I went to an exhibition in the Royal Academy. That splendid museum is in a part of London that glows with wealth. Three portraits on the outside of the building advertise the exhibition. They were of Vincent van Gogh, Paul Cézanne and L S Lowry. To me it seemed somewhat ironic to see three such outsiders celebrated in such fashionable surroundings.

Lowry was luckier than van Gogh and Cézanne: he was a shy and lonely man but he received some recognition late in his life. Van Gogh seemed born to be an outsider: he failed as a student and a teacher and as an art dealer – and, in the eyes of the world, as an artist. In the popular image, he was a wild man, an incorrigible rebel. The reality could hardly have been more different.

Vincent was born into the middle class and, in his heart, never really left it. He longed for a regular job and a home and a wife and a family – it wasn't to be. One day while painting in a field near a village in northern France, he shot himself in the chest with a revolver. He was an expert in anatomy and knew that the wound wasn't fatal. It was a cry for help. Next day, he was sitting up in bed, smoking his pipe and conversing lucidly. However, he had neglected his health so badly that the wound festered and he died.

Cézanne was pathologically shy. He made few, if any, friends in his many years as an artist in Paris. Sometimes he went to a café frequented by writers and artists and assorted intellectuals, but he always remained on the edge of the company and rarely spoke. He spent the last few years of his life in his hometown in Provence. He was just as much an outsider there: he had inherited great wealth, but he dressed like a tramp so that he could paint in the open. His wealthy neighbours deplored his way of life, though he wasn't totally an outsider: a local group of young intellectuals idolised him.

This was a compensation that Gerard Manley Hopkins did not enjoy. He taught Greek in the new university in Dublin in the early years of the twentieth century. He had no sympathy with Irish nationalism and made no friends in the city. He passed through Dublin like a ghost. His order, the Jesuits, refused him permission to publish his poetry. He was, in every sense, an outsider. He pined away with loneliness like the subject of William Cowper's poem 'The Castaway' – he was out of humanity's reach. Society can do little in such cases.

Con Houlihan

TWO PEOPLE'S LIVES INSPIRED BY OUTSIDERS

TIM HYDE AND GERALDINE MCAULIFFE

People come in all shapes and sizes. There are no norms, and there are no standards. We are all different, and yet to be different means we become outsiders.

Gerry and I have both become outsiders because we see something special in the people that society has difficulty with, the people we meet each and every day. We work for very different organisations, and yet we are united in our thinking, we are united as outsiders.

All of us have a need to be heard.
All of us have a need to be recognised.
All of us need to be loved.

These might seem to be very obvious statements, and the fact is they are. However, do we really understand them? Do we realise that our world would be so much better if we really listened to what they are saying to us?

Tim

I knew Mary for only a short period of time, and yet she comes to mind frequently as I work in and around St Patrick's Cathedral in Dublin with people from all walks of life. She was a tall, dark and very pretty young woman who had everything to live for. Her smile would light up the room, and yet she was an outsider. She didn't conform to the norms of society.

Mary was a very special person who helped me to better understand why I am here. She helped me to see that there is always hope in the midst of despair, no matter how great the despair.

I met her on the general medical ward of a very busy city hospital. Mary had anorexia nervosa and was gradually wasting away. The doctors and nurses had tried to help her gain weight and they had tried to ease her pain, but to no avail.

As I listened to her story, I could feel the pain in her voice. She so wanted to get better and yet nothing the doctors said or did seemed to help her.

Mary spoke about her family, she spoke about her friends, and she opened her heart up to me, so that I might understand. As I listened, the battle inside her head became more and more apparent. Here was a very intelligent young woman who knew how to make herself better, and yet she was losing the battle. She couldn't beat the constant barrage of negativity inside her mind. She needed help.

We spoke about the irrational thoughts going round inside her head, and about the need for her to be understood. 'Do you know,' she said, 'you're the first person that understands me.' These words still haunt me today. Did she really mean what she said? Was I really the first person that understood her? Or was I, perhaps, the first person that really listened to her?

Mary knew what she wanted. She knew how best she could be helped at this time. The language used in treating her caused her problems. Words like 'weight' and 'fat' meant that she couldn't eat, because if she did, she would become someone she couldn't cope with. 'If only they would use different words,' she said, 'words like "goodness", and "energy", I would be able to fight back.' She had a plan, 'Would you help me write a letter to the doctor explaining this?' she said.

Later that day, the letter was written and Mary waited with expectation. She had taken responsibility for her life. She had decided that today would be the day when she would begin to fight back. 'Pray that they listen,' she said, as I left her on the ward that day.

When I next visited Mary the following day, I found to my distress that she had discharged herself, and left no forwarding address. 'She was messing us about,' one nurse said. 'She had no intention of getting better.' I knew otherwise. Mary had tried to put her point across, and she hadn't been listened to. She had lost hope in the system, and had once again found herself to be the outsider. Nobody understood. Nobody listened.

Was there no hope for someone like Mary?

Later that year, I received a Christmas card. It said, 'Just a short note to say thank you for visiting me and also for being so understanding.'

Mary hadn't given up hope. She was now in a different hospital in a different part of the country. She was still fighting. 'I'm psychologically struggling,' she said, 'despite knowing that I need to gain weight to have life. I hope it will eventually become easier – it's this hope that keeps me going, but it's frequently fading now.'

It saddens me to think that that was the last time I heard from Mary, and yet she changed my outlook on life. She made me a better person. She helped me to see that everyone has a need to be heard. Everyone has a need to be recognised for who we are, and all of us need to be loved.

Mary added a little footnote to her card, it read: '"Life is a journey not a destination" (anon).' Sadly for her, the journey had been fraught with pain and suffering, and that's the case for so many of our outsiders and yet, she still had hope that one day the journey would become easier.

The outsiders in our world are so often the people who say the things we don't want to hear, and yet we need to hear what they have to say.

Gerry

I think the reason I can identify with outsiders is because I was once the outsider myself.

In the early 1970s, I lost a child. My baby boy died. In those days, nobody talked about things like that, nobody came near me in hospital and, when I came out of hospital and went home, even my family and friends didn't know what to say. I could feel that they were uncomfortable around me. I could feel their embarrassment. I too felt uncomfortable and embarrassed around them. I remember how it made me feel angry, and there seemed to be no release. All in all, it was a very unpleasant time in my life.

My experience of being made to feel uncomfortable and embarrassed, even excluded, ties in with the feelings of so many of the people with whom I work.

Take for instance Jim and his girlfriend who came in after St Patrick's Day, upset because people had obviously moved away from them. He recalled how a little girl had said to her mother, 'Mommy that man stinks.'

Jim was not his normal boisterous self. He was unusually quiet that morning. The incident had hurt him.

Jim, like so many of the men and women we see, was made to feel unwanted. We regularly struggle as we try to persuade people with sometimes serious injuries or diseases to visit the local A&E department. Even there they are made to feel different.

How often do we miss out by not getting to know the outsiders around us? I'm reminded of a few of the men who come in to Trust on a regular basis. Take for instance Bill who comes in out of the cold to get a wash and cleanup, and possibly some clean, dry clothes, who, when asked how he's doing, always replies 'fantastic'. You see, he is always cheerful, always courteous, and always thankful for the little we do for him. He's an inspiration to us all. Then there's Joe, who struggled with his addiction to alcohol over all the years we knew him. He never gave up seeking sobriety. He was always optimistic that one day he would succeed. He loved to be smart and would always want the designer labels. He sadly died at the age of thirty-four. Or how about John who comes in to us and who is wheelchair bound? Whenever he comes in, he always gives us a gift of ₤5 before he leaves, so that, at the end of the day, we can relax over a decent cup of coffee, one made for us. You see these people are not the dregs of society, they are just people who live different lives to us. Yes, they may have problems. Yes, they may have addictions but, at the end of the day, how different are they really?

Our stories are very different, and yet they have united us in our understanding of the outsider.

The outsiders are people just like you and me. We all live in a society that shows little care or thought for hurting people. They are special people who can be an inspiration to us all, if for no other reason than because they survive against all the odds. The challenge for us all is to find ways of engaging with the outsider so that we can learn from them.

We would just like to say thank you to all the outsiders we know for allowing us to share their lives, and for making us better people.

Tim Hyde and Geraldine McAuliffe

THE BEST LESSON

MIRANDA IVEAGH

When I was seven, my parents moved house from south-east England to northeast Scotland. My grandfather had given them an eccentric property, a fifteenth-century un-inhabited castle with an appendage of land and houses including an octagonal building with a central courtyard and pepperpot turrets. This was to be my new home. The empty castle was to be my new school.

My mama had arranged for lessons to be given to me in one of the first floor anterooms decorated in a red patterned wallpaper and, appropriately, called the Peacock Parlour.

Miss McPherson duly arrived to instruct her charge and brought with her exciting lined copybooks with pictures of thistles on the covers, new pencils and rubbers and an array of textbooks full of new slants on old themes, so Flora MacDonald and Robert the Bruce came into my world.

Miss McPherson wore the scent of lavender and gentle violet-coloured tweed. She wrote in exquisite copperplate and was methodical and kind. She taught in a disciplined and precise way and I probably took great strides in this one-to-one, lonely method of education; even the tick of the clock seemed invasive, but it was comforting and she was an enthralling teacher.

We rarely went outside together, as she would appear in the morning in her old beige Austin car and disappear into the early-afternoon darkness of the countryside, I knew not where. She gave me a Bible for Christmas.

As time went by, my parents would go away for several days at a time leaving me at home with a baby brother and the limit of regular nursery life arranged severely by Nanny Sutherland with starch in her apron and not much time for an older sister.

I began to see my castle education and Miss Mc-Pherson's Austin as my passport to the great outside world. I implored my parents to allow my governess to take me to the local, but distant, village while they were away, to buy cards, embroidery cotton or to visit the leather-scented shop of the cobbler.

Such shock was to come. Normally friendly people averted their gaze; there were no greetings from people I recognised as familiar. I noticed my parents' normally genial acquaintances avoiding our path. Miss McPherson kept our conversation flowing, her head held high, clasping my hand tightly, but nobody hailed us as they would have hailed my mother or father.

I drank in the slight to us both as I identified with my mentor in my childish way. I felt the pain of ostracism and admired her outward armour, as she remained calm and unbowed, ever-polite, quietly composed and seemingly unafraid, even of the cobbler Mr Shand's frigid stare.

I never found out the cause of this evident unpopularity as my parents never enlightened me and now it is too late to ask. The quaint two-man school ended after two terms, leaving one sad student, who still thinks of her tutor with awe and admiration today. She taught me some lessons that were more than academic; they were valuable lessons for life, to keep a broad mind, to revere the eccentric and to honour the outsider.

Miranda Iveagh

THE OUTSIDER

MICHAEL KAVANAGH

I know him well. I don't know him at all. Even after twenty-five years, that's how I feel. I work on the street so you can be sure very little escapes my notice. I would consider myself very streetwise with a good insight into human nature but I haven't cracked this one. It was twenty-five years ago when first I met 'the outsider'. Along he came and stood in front of me and said, 'You f****** asshole.' That was my introduction to him. Those expletives might be common enough nowadays, but twenty-five years ago, even I was taken aback. I don't know where he came from, or why I was targeted.

This outsider – James is what I will call him – will probably be known to most Dubliners. A bit like 'Bang Bang' if you like.

What can I tell you about James. He can be a contradiction. Eccentric yet normal at times, religious yet blasphemous, intelligent and respectful. Why the contradiction you might ask? I don't know. I can only suppose because, even after twenty-five years of nearly daily contact with him, I know very little about him. Is it society that has him the way he is, I wonder? Often, he will refer to himself as a beggar, 'I'm just a dirty old beggar. I'm homeless and I'll always remain homeless.' One day I said to him, 'Don't you have friends?'

'Yes,' he said. 'Only for a few people in the world like you who introduce me to people who understand me, I think because they are always respectful towards me and don't look at me like a beggar but look at me like a human being.' How sad is that?

My daily contact with James starts at about six o'clock in the morning. By this hour, he has risen from this rest place. He arrives on the street and gets his daily paper, actually two of them, which he always pays for. He sits down on his night bed, which he carries on his shoulder, and reads aloud the whole three pages of the sporting commentary in detail and he won't be very quiet about it either, but very entertaining. To me, I think he lets off steam this way. He would have his half-hour with me then he would head to the Salvation Army in York Street for a wash and shave.

James looked after his daily toilet in the men's toilet in Stephen's Green. He later moved to the Salvation Army in York Street until it closed. For someone as fastidious as James, cleanliness is, and always was, very important. So we needed to find another facility to allow for his daily cleaning ritual. James approached me for help. Since I know people in the area, I considered the possibilities and decided to prevail upon the good people of Bruxelles public house in Harry Street. The Egan family have been more than kind. James can now use the pub's private bathroom and, when he emerges from there to face the day, all clean and tidy, he finds a hot cup of coffee waiting for him. James is extremely grateful for this kindness.

But what happens to James for the rest of the day? Some of it can be filled in. I know he is based in the same area all the time and his day follows a routine. After his morning toilet, he moves off to the centre of Grafton Street where he pontificates at the top of his voice outside Clarendon Street church where many of his 'friends' and 'supporters' attend mass. These would be the people who help finance his existence. Later, he moves to O'Connell Street, where you will find him sitting on one of the monuments listening to his radio and rambling on to anyone who will listen to him. Funny thing, if you are ever passing and he should spot you, he will always bid you good evening. His last stop, where he beds down for the night, is the entrance to the Masonic Lodge in Molesworth Street, where the porter kindly makes him a nightcap.

How can a man live that sort of life? James never gets close to you, when he is talking to you, but converses from a distance. I find that strange. It suggests to me a fear of human contact. I would like to get closer to him, but think this unlikely. If it hasn't happened in twenty-five years how is it going to happen now? But I do have the greatest respect for this man, because behind him, and despite all his shouting and bawling, there is a great heart and a good will. But I think society let him down somewhere along the way. But whether me or my friends will ever get through to him, God only knows.

I spoke earlier of James referring to himself as a beggar. This is not strictly true.

He does play the mouth organ so you could say he plays for his supper. And he has his regular fan club who support him. One man in particular, whom I shall refer to as 'the solicitor' because, even though I know him for over twenty years, I don't know his name or even if he is a solicitor. Anyway, he contributes daily to James's coffers. Asking after James's health, he slips me some funds for him and, at Christmas time, there is always a bit extra. Anyway, one day we were chatting about James. He knows James is getting older and finding it more difficult to exist on the streets. So he suggested to me, knowing I was well connected in the area, that if I could find accommodation for James, he would willingly foot the bill. He sees James as a bit mad in one sense but would rather have him at his table than some of the supposed sane people he has had to entertain in his life.

I believe there are others in the life of James, like this

kind man, that I'm not aware of. I don't know what is going to happen to him. He doesn't drink or smoke or do drugs. He is harmless. An innocent really. I know he is getting older and we both know the streets are more dangerous than when first he set up his bed under the portico of the Masonic Hall in Molesworth Street. He has been attacked, urinated on and set fire to. He is afraid. What is to become of him?

Michael Kavanagh

LISTEN

Toenail cracked with stories of a life
Shelling a flesh that walked a thousand years
Unclimbed rock face of this mountain man

Clothes suburban-less
Not homeless
Ringed by wild fumes

Whiskers an ivy climbing on
Cathedral mouth
Foaming seas–praying words

Eyes fathomless hosts
To love buried beneath
Remember that courting boy

A hospital somewhere
Violent blows rained on innocence
Eyes retracted now

I am gifted to see that landscape
The flying fugue of voice
A cadence coming to rest

Waves deep and true
Still silent sounding
Listen

Eamon Keane

This poem was written after Eamon produced a programme with Vincent Browne in Trust for RTÉ Radio 1.

AN HONOURABLE MAN

GRAINNE KENNY

When I was asked by Alice Leahy to write a piece for this book, there was no question of me not doing it; equally there was no question of who it would be about – Eric Smyth. The fact that Alice's request fell on my desk just as I returned from a study visit to drug-treatment centres in the south of Ireland with the good reverend only strengthened my determination to tell his story.

The reason for the visit was a request from the Drugs Sub-Committee of Belfast City Council. This cross-party committee was formed and chaired by councillor, the Rev Eric Smyth, a former Lord Mayor of Belfast and member of the DUP.

I first met Eric in London in 1995, just prior to his official installation as Lord Mayor. The occasion was a London Conference of European Mayors exploring ways to co-operate in the fight against drugs. I had been lobbying city mayors across Europe to attend this conference and, in the process, telephoned Belfast City Hall. The response from an official was swift and to the point. 'The new Lord Mayor would definitely not be interested.' Undeterred, I wrote a personal letter to the new Lord Mayor. Still no response.

On arrival in London, I enquired if Belfast was listed to attend. This time the response was in the affirmative. When the party arrived, I approached him and, hand outstretched, said, 'You're welcome Lord Mayor – I'm the woman from Dublin!'

Thus began a deep friendship with a truly decent man whose strength of character and wonderful, northern humour has enriched so many lives, including my own.

Eric Smyth began his life in the working-class Belfast of the 1950s. He hated school and used every opportunity to 'mitch'. Having been told by his teacher, 'Smyth, you will never get anywhere in life', Eric lost all interest in schooling. What was not recognised then was that the young boy was dyslexic. While he could understand what the teachers were saying, he could not write it down and had been labelled as ESN, or educationally sub-normal. His classmates used to tease him and call him stupid. So his days were usually taken up with art, cricket and football. Girls were also high on his agenda! At fourteen, he went to hear a preacher, Rev Paisley, speak at his church and the seeds were sown for Eric to ask what was needed from him to be 'saved'. Although he didn't know it at the time, this was the beginning of a pattern that would change his life completely.

At fifteen, Eric left school to work on a mushroom farm. He then began attending the Free Presbyterian Church regularly and, in the early 1960s, was to be found proclaiming his Christian message at the gates of Belfast City Hall. It was there that he met his soulmate, Frances Swaffield from Sandy Row. In six months they became engaged, and married shortly after. The happy couple set up home in a tiny house with no bathroom, only an outside toilet. They started their family there and Eric continued 'evangelising'.

During those very happy years, despite a lack of money, Eric began to sense that his prayers and ambitions were slowly being answered. With persistence, there were certain word patterns that he would recognise. It could not be described as reading, but he was beginning to challenge his dyslexia and piece together enough words to allow him to understand. With a growing family to feed, the wages from mushroom picking were becoming inadequate and Eric moved to a job checking tyres in a factory. The escalating troubles in the early 1970s meant that security guards were needed at all access points to the main shopping areas, so Eric found a way to earn extra money for the growing family. At the same time, he was preaching the Christian message to anyone who would listen.

Eric was, by now, dedicated to his faith and wanted to serve Christ full time. His dyslexia meant that he had to leave his studies at a Christian College in Belfast, although he did eventually travel to Singapore to be ordained by a Christian Church.

Politics

In 1979, Eric finally left his job to begin full-time preaching. He took charge of a little Outreach Mission Hall in Sandy Row – The Jesus Saves Mission. After some time, he began to sense that, for social as well as moral reasons, committed Christians should be involved in local politics. He realised that his 'flock' was genuinely concerned about more mundane matters. For example, basic sanitary conditions in their homes, the state of the footpaths and matters that affected their everyday lives. In 1981, he was invited to stand as a candidate for the May elections to the City Council. It was during this period of his life – calling to houses and listening to the concerns of people trying to cope and raise their families, sometimes under terrible conditions – that he and Frances began to foster children who needed the care of a loving home.

Throughout the years, Eric, Frances and their six kids shared their home with over thirty foster children – adopting three special children: Matthew, who has spina bifida and is confined to a wheelchair, Donika and, more recently, Kirsty. Like Donika, Kirsty is a special child needing a lot of time and energy. I have never heard

Frances or Eric complain and the teamwork in that loving and extremely happy home is staggering. It is a home filled with compassion and laughter.

So, in 1981, the hard slog that is the reality of a politician's life began in earnest for Eric, the fundamentalist preacher. Balancing his pastoral and church duties with his growing family, door-to-door canvassing, planning and policy meetings – while struggling with his lack of formal education coupled with dyslexia – was adding a whole new dimension to the Smyth family life. On 20th May, Rev Eric Smyth the student, labelled as a no-hoper, was elected to Belfast City Council.

He now had to face the challenge of devising his own system of compensations because of his lack of formal education, to deal with policy documents and debates in City Hall.

As a newly elected city councillor, Eric opened an office and advice centre in his house. The bush telegraph on the Shankill spread the word rapidly. This was a fundamentalist Christian minister turned politician who really cared about people's problems.

However, such dedication to duty inevitably has its price and, today, Eric says that he regrets the fact that he was away from his family too much and, if he had his life over, would not make the same mistake.

Two of his sons were arrested and charged with drug dealing when he was elected Lord Mayor. The family was in a state of deep shock. They never realised that the personality changes that were occurring very gradually in their boys were drug related. In this they were no different to any family caught in such a situation. Something was happening to them, something that neither Frances nor Eric understood. Understandably, raising kids in those troubled times in Belfast was not easy for anyone. Their own home had been bombed and the Troubles made life for everyone very dysfunctional.

Now, those two boys who had always been so pleasant at home and fun to live with were becoming highly unpleasant and even nasty. Doors were kicked and furniture was hammered on. Shouting and yelling became part of their nature. The verbal abuse of their mother who loved them so much was becoming too much for Eric to tolerate. Finally, one night he made a painful decision. He put them out of the house. The problem with the boys, they had learned, was drugs. Both using and selling.

In 1994, both boys were sent to Magilligan Prison. Their parents were distraught. Night after night, they sat up either in bed or in the kitchen drinking tea asking themselves, 'Where did we go wrong?' Later the boys reassured them that, as parents, they had not failed them. They told Eric and Frances, that it was their own fault they had wound up in jail.

It was a heart-rending period for the family as, at this time, there were public appearances to be made – either in Eric's political life or as a minister in his church. There was one thing however, that they both agreed on and that was that, although their hearts were breaking, they were glad that the boys had been arrested before they killed someone else's son or spread the misery of drug addiction to someone else's family.

While their friends rallied round them, the most-cruel taunts came from members of the paramilitary groups. They would jeer at Eric as he drove his Mission Bus around the streets of Belfast. During those depressing times, two things proved to be a great source of comfort to Eric and Frances. The first was the support of so many people from all sections of the community and many shades of political and religious persuasion. Also the media. They admired the sheer honesty of Eric as he unreservedly denounced drug taking and dealing, condeming his sons for what they had done while never wavering in his love for them as a father. Mark and Keith, having served their prison terms, are now released and finished with drug taking. They are once again leading full lives. Both are lovely young men with warm smiles of welcome when we meet in their parents' home.

Lord Mayor

It was during those turbulent years that the Rev Eric Smyth was proposed for the office of Lord Mayor of Belfast. The suggestion met with ridicule from some of his fellow councillors, according to Eric. Outright hostility from others.

For instance, as a DUP man, they suggested he would not meet with Catholics. Others cast doubt on the ability of a man who was dyslexic and still had trouble reading unfamiliar texts. How could such a man hold such an important office they asked? Although he had the support of the Unionist Party, that was not enough and, according to Eric, he prayed and prayed about it. The month of May 1995 was spent seeking the support of various councillor friends. Others laughed at the prospect of a semi-literate, 'good-living' DUP Lord Mayor.

Eric had the last laugh, however, and was elected against all the odds.

To demonstrate his desire to serve all sections of the community in his city, Alasdair McDonald of the SDLP was appointed Deputy Lord Mayor. Those people who said that it would never work were proved wrong. Many who said that a fundamentalist DUP councillor would never be accepted by a high percentage of the citizens of Belfast, were also proved wrong. Eric's dignity and grace in the face of his detractors won the respect he deserved.

Charity Work

When elected to be Lord Mayor, Eric chose spina bifida as the theme charity for his term in office. He pledged himself to raising money to help parents who couldn't afford the special, and very expensive, wheelchairs for their severely handicapped children. The committee that he set up worked extremely hard, encouraged by his enthusiasm. The appearance of the magnetic Matthew on a number of public occasions has brought home to the public the sheer extent of the disability.

I was delighted (as a southern Roman Catholic) to have been invited by Eric to his inauguration in City Hall and, later, as his guest at the Lord Mayor's Fund-raising Ball. Having entered into the enthusiasm of it all, I had managed to do my share of fundraising south of the border. Mine was done with the idea of out-stretched hands across the border. I approached hotels, guest houses and farmhouses for weekend breaks with dinner to be auctioned at the ball. The response was generous and I felt a great pride to be present during the draw and to hear the peals of delight when names were called to collect a voucher for a farmhouse holiday in County Sligo or a weekend for two in the Conrad Hotel in Dublin, among others. The great joke of the night was when Frances, the Lord Mayor's wife, won a weekend for two in a lovely hotel in Athlone, but had to give it back to be drawn again. It would not have been considered polite to keep the prize. Poor Frances!

Anti-Drugs Campaign

During his term of office, as well as supporting the cause of spina bifida, Eric opened his doors and his home to me. I regularly stayed at his house and visited his church in the Limestone Road, where I was welcomed by eve-ryone and always invited back. Together they shared in prayers for my husband who was ill and I always felt that I was among friends. During that time, Belfast City Hall became almost like a home from home to me. Eric's driver ferried me around the city visiting different communities from the Falls to the Shankill. Nothing was too much trouble. Listening to their problems and sharing information, we organised, with Eric's help, exchange visits between Belfast and Dublin.

Bill Clinton

When Eric was advised that the American president was to visit Belfast in November 1995, his first question was, 'Could he switch on the Christmas tree lights outside City Hall?' The Mayor of Nashville had sent a tree. The president's handlers invited Eric to share the platform and advised him that he had one minute to speak. Eric replied that one minute would not be enough as he wanted to give the American president a really good Belfast welcome. So the dyslexic man, who was scared of all the formalities of office, was given the time to address the most powerful man in the world and to give a really warm welcome to the visitors to his native city. But first, he calmly asked that they would pray together. Afterwards, Mr Clinton told him how touched he had felt that the eyes of the world had focused on this scene in Belfast.

Dublin Visit

It was at this time that Dublin had as its Lord Mayor Councillor Sean 'Dublin Bay Rockall' Loftus. Sean Loftus, too, was a man who could be described as an outsider. A conservationist who was not afraid to be different, to stand out from the crowd. A truly delightful man and a devout Christian too. Since the founding

of the State, Dublin had never had a visit from a Lord
Mayor of Belfast. Having no political ties myself, I was
perhaps in the ideal situation to suggest such a visit.
The suggestion was warmly greeted by Sean, although
slightly more cautiously by Eric. Although willing, his
lack of formal education was worrying him.

Then, on one beautiful snowy day in November 1995,
the black Daimler bearing the DUP Lord Mayor of
Belfast and his wife drew up at the Dublin Mansion
House and a little bit of history was made. Over lunch,
the two men chatted like old friends. They both discovered their mutual interest in spina bifida and a shared
love of the Christian message. As they laughed and
talked, Sean's wife Una firmly told her husband that his
soup was getting cold, much to the amusement of his
guests. Later that year, I had the honour to receive an
award from the Lord Mayor of Dublin. I asked if it
would be all right for me to invite the Smyths. To their
great delight, the Loftuses invited them to sleep over in
the Mansion House as their guests.

Since then, Eric has visited Dublin on many occasions to study our drug problems and to meet with families in the inner city. The warmth he engenders in everyone he meets is a joy to behold. He has also met inner-city drug activists from Sinn Féin.

When his time in office as Lord Mayor was finished,
Eric persuaded Belfast City Council to form a drugs
sub-committee and he was elected as its chairman. It is
cross party and I can attest to the fact that all co-operate
to fight drugs and engage in study visits here in Ireland
and further afield in Europe.

Eric, for his part, has lobbied in the European Parliament against voting to support drug legislation in an
upcoming debate.

In 2001, Belfast City Hall hosted the Lord Mayor's
Cities Against Drugs Conference. Delegates came from

Scandinavia and Russia as well as The Netherlands, Italy and other European countries.

Eric Smyth, the man that I had been told would certainly have no interest in coming to that London conference eight years previously, has been appointed to the Board of European Cities Against Drugs and is, in 2003, involved in planning its tenth anniversary conference in Stockholm.

Grainne Kenny

KARL'S CHOICES

GENE KERRIGAN

You could tell straightaway that Karl Crawley was a spoofer. No doubt there was some nugget of truth at the heart of the story he told – he'd been in jail, he'd had a hard enough life – but he couldn't resist spoofing his story to an absurd level. Like the way he talked about the time he decided to break out of Mountjoy.

The way Karl told it, he carved a fake gun out of a paperback book and blackened it with boot polish so it looked like a Colt .45. And he used it to hold up the screws and make them release him from his cell.

Obviously pure fiction, but he told the story casually, downplaying the dramatics, making fun of himself. Editor Vincent Browne introduced me to Karl at the offices of *Magill* magazine, where I worked back in 1980. He suggested I might see if we could maybe publish something about Karl's life in jail and out.

As Karl told his stories, including the one about the fake gun, I listened and nodded and said that was very interesting, and quietly decided he was telling me something he'd seen in a movie. Back then, Karl had the looks and the swagger of the young Paul Newman. His stories might be remarkable, but they were so obviously a mixture of fact and fantasy that it would be impossible to sort out the truth from the spoofing.

We met a second and third time and, one day, Karl casually handed over a bunch of documents – court, prison and medical records. The detail in the records was immense, and it backed up every twist and turn of his story. That thing about holding up the prison guards with the paperback 'gun' – it was all there in a report in the prison records. And Karl could even remember the title of the book from which he carved the gun.

Karl spent a lot of time in jail, and in worse places. The psychiatric name they put on him was sociopath. No sense of conscience. Not to be trusted. Oddly enough, thinking back over twenty years, I can't identify a single lie that Karl told me. Not about himself, anyway, not about his extraordinary life.

The first time he went to jail, in 1969, Karl was just short of his seventeenth birthday. It wasn't the first time he was locked up. That happened when he was three months old. One of twelve kids, father gone to England, mother coping as best she could, she had to ask the State to take some of the burden.

That was in 1952, and we know how conscientiously the State took its responsibilities in those days. Karl's story, as he progressed from the custody of the nuns in an orphanage to the custody of the Christian Brothers in Glasnevin, was one that has become wearily familiar. The beatings, the Brother with the wandering hands, the harshness of under-resourced facilities where fear was part of the curriculum. The sheer lack of love and care from overworked, under-trained staff who struggled to do the State's job, while harvesting souls for their god. All but a few months of Karl's first nine years were spent in orphanages. Then he was in and out of a special school for a while, and he finally shrugged off that world at the age of twelve, sleeping rough on the streets of Dublin.

By then, Karl had learned well the lesson that violence works. They want you to do something, they tell you, and if you don't do it they hit you. And if you hit back, they hit you harder and, if you keep hitting back, you'll get a right hammering, but make a big enough nuisance of yourself and they may back off.

Moving into his teens, Karl lived on Dublin's northside, sometimes with his ma, whom he loved and who loved him. I know she loved him because I talked to someone who knew her back then. I know he loved her because he talked lovingly about her, years later. That love survived in such circumstances is one of the little miracles of Karl's life.

There were other tough kids in the area, and when they saw Karl coming they crossed the street, stayed out of his way. Already, Karl had a reputation.

In that mid-1960s period, as Karl went into his teens, no one's employment prospects were great. And Karl's were next to non-existent. He got occasional jobs, but discipline was a problem. People telling him to do things, and the way they told him. Treat Karl as an equal, that was cool. Treat him disrespectfully and you got a cold stare. Push him too hard, Karl could tell you to fuck off with a contemptuous drawl that made each word a sentence in itself. 'Fuck. Off.'

He lost one job when the boss told him to wash his Jaguar. Wanting to do a good job, Karl got out the tin of Vim scouring powder, which did wonders for the paint.

Karl's choices were limited. There were few niches into which a working-class teenager with little education, few social skills, a battered self-image and a wide streak of rebelliousness could fit. He could settle down to a dole existence, picking up odd jobs now and then. Which meant never having money, never having a nice flat, doing without television or records (Karl was into Bob Dylan and could knowledgeably discuss his songs), cool clothes, the drinking sessions and the dancing and the holidays – all the things that were becoming standard pleasures as Ireland began discarding its provincialism.

Or he could take what he wanted, when he could.

Karl started off with the same average intelligence

and abilities given to the rest of us. Circumstances dras-
tically limited what he could do with them. By his teens,
Karl didn't have the temperament to fit into any open-
ings society might allow him; he didn't have the ambi-
tion to become a big-time criminal. He had talents. He
was strong, muscular. He could climb up pipes, in
through windows. He could jump over counters.

Karl liked nice clothes. He'd visit the city-centre stores
– Roches, Bolger's, wherever – come home with powder-
blue jeans, a smart jacket, whatever he fancied. He'd
shoplift for things he didn't need – 'Picnic knives,' he
laughed later, 'what did I want fucking picnic knives for?'
He'd spot an open window in a house, up and in. Karl
was so good at climbing, he'd find a way up to windows
others wouldn't dare attempt. Whatever you find, throw
it out the window to your mate down below. Then, out
and down and off to sell the stuff.

With the petty crime came drinking and drugs. You
want drink, smash the window of an off-licence, grab a
few bottles and run. You want uppers or downers, reds,
blues, yellow jackets, whatever, you burgle a chemist
shop. Karl's ambitions narrowed down to where he was
going to get the next handful of barbs from.

There was a price to be paid. Jail was an occupational
hazard, but that was all right. Karl had little to lose. There
was never going to be a big job, lots of money. There
would never be a car or a house. There was never going
to be a happy ending. Choice: mooch from one dead-
end to the next – yes sir, no sir – or do it the way he
knew how to, and take the consequences.

Karl got the usual chances. Warnings, probation, then
– three months before his seventeenth birthday – they
put him in St Patrick's Prison for young offenders. A
six-month stretch, for fourteen counts of housebreaking, and before long he was on report and the governor

was telling him, 'I bet you never thought there was a place like this.'

Years later, Karl chuckled when he talked about that. *Place like this.* The places Karl had been, the governor couldn't dream of.

For Karl, jail was somewhere they tested your will, your strength. Choice: keep your head down, do as you're told, do smart time, get a couple of months off for good behaviour, or respond as Karl had always responded to being pushed around. Push back.

In September 1969, Karl Crawley climbed onto the roof of St Patrick's. He was protesting about something – he couldn't remember the detail later, but he knew he was depressed. He'd gone into jail for the first time in January; he got out in July and, in September, he was back inside, another housebreaking deal. When they got him down from the roof, they declared him insane and sent him off to Dundrum Mental Hospital.

Karl wasn't insane. The Drum wasn't an appropriate place for a disturbed boy, but the system didn't know what else to do with a kid who kicked back, who wouldn't show deference, who didn't fit in.

The Drum was like St Patrick's, but with extra restraints and tranquillisers. He wasn't insane, but he wasn't deferring to authority and settling into his place in the scheme of things, so maybe the Drum would put manners on him.

Karl's response was to climb onto the roof, an escape attempt. When they sent him back to St Pat's, they put him in a cell in the basement and Karl took a metal spoon and broke the bowl off and swallowed the handle. Fuck. You.

It was a strange, but effective, way of exerting some control over a situation where the system was determined to make him see that he had no control, that he was at its mercy. When Karl swallowed the spoon, they had to take him to the Mater Hospital. Subjected to overwhelming force, he had found a way of saying no.

He did it again. And again. They put him in solitary. They wouldn't let him near a spoon. He began swallowing other things. A battery, a bit of a bedspring, a piece off a ventilator grill.

Karl paid a heavy price. He had to have an operation to remove metal from his stomach. Complications followed, he spent four months in hospital and shrank to less than six stone. After he got out of prison, he stole a car, ended up in Mountjoy and was declared insane and sent to the Drum, from which he made a prison break on Christmas Day 1970. He went home to his ma.

He was caught, of course, a few weeks later, and 1971 was more of the same and, on Christmas Day 1971, a rooftop protest ended with another swallowing incident, another operation, and they declared him insane again and sent him to the Drum. For three months, he was kept in his cell for twenty-four hours a day, pumped full of drugs. They laced his food with so much Serenace that he shuffled around like an old man and, by the time he got sent back to jail, his motor function was gone and they had to teach him how to walk. He was just twenty years of age.

This kind of thing went on for five years. By 1973, the doctors were telling Karl he was risking his life, swallowing metal, it was dangerous to keep on operating. He'd had so many operations his abdomen was a mass of scars.

A pattern was established. Petty crime, usually for drugs, chemist shops, whatever – three months in the Joy, a month out, a month in, two months out. Conflict with the screws, off to the Drum. Karl was allocated his own high-security cell in the basement of Mountjoy and he was sent there any time he was convicted. The petty criminal, in for nicking a handful of Mandrax, was rubbing shoulders with the dangerous types, the UDA heavies and those whose crimes were so repulsive they couldn't mix with ordinary decent criminals.

It was down in the Base that Karl carved a gun from a paperback book entitled *Yoga and Religion* and conned his way out of the cell and, maybe if one of the heavies hadn't laughed at Karl's hard neck, the screws wouldn't have jumped him. It wasn't long before he was back in the Drum.

Karl wasn't insane – and a consultant psychiatrist would later state categorically, 'Karl Crawley is not insane' – but, over the course of five years or so, he was declared insane twelve times, an average of over twice a year. It gave the State the right to drug him into submission. And each time they released him from the Drum, they had to sign a form saying he was no longer insane. Later on, Karl got a good laugh out of that. 'The only man in Ireland with twelve certificates of sanity.'

At any stage, Karl could have bowed the head, backed off; they'd have got the message. But Karl's choices were now extremely narrow – the one way he could assert his existence as an individual was to kick back, to say no, to cause trouble, to thresh and scream and struggle as they tried to make him be quiet.

In the outside world, around that time, *One Flew Over the Cuckoo's Nest* was a celebrated novel and a multimillion dollar movie, and they were handing Jack Nicholson an Oscar for pretending to be an inmate who wouldn't conform to the rules of a mental hospital. In the real world, the reward for that kind of thing was somewhat less glamorous.

Eventually, Karl's screams found sympathetic ears on the outside, the Prisoners' Rights Organisation got involved. Compassionate lawyers took up his case and, by the mid-1970s, the State stopped declaring him insane, and Karl finally stopped swallowing pieces of metal. The High Court and the Supreme Court became involved and the State had to watch its manners. Psychiatrists told the courts that Karl wasn't the only young man who was disturbed and rebellious but not insane, that there were up to twenty at that time and a specialised unit was needed.

The courts couldn't order the State to build such a unit, but everyone knew that it wouldn't be long in coming. That was 1976.

Karl's law-breaking – always petty stuff – continued, as did the short sentences. In total, Karl served far longer than anyone caught for a major crime, longer than people who got rich from their crimes, even people who badly damaged other people.

He took drugs, he got drunk, he got into fights. One day in the mid-1980s, I winced at a gash on his hand, and he waved away my concern. It was like he'd forgotten about the injury until I drew attention to it. 'Just a thing, you know, fella with a knife, I grabbed the knife.'

The doctors told him that his scarred abdomen was a potential breeding ground for serious diseases. There were times when he didn't look after himself and the wounds on his stomach opened, festered, and you could get the smell from several feet away.

Karl found happiness for a while; he had a personal life. And by and by, in the mid-1980s, the anger seemed to ebb. For all the State threw at him, he hadn't been broken, but he came to some kind of draw. His body was so ravaged, he was considered to be disabled and they gave him a bus pass.

For eleven years, Karl stayed out of trouble, then he was caught nicking a pile of jeans. He went inside and they did a medical and gave him the bad news and Karl

– who'd never lost his fondness for drugs – said, 'When you're locked you get careless.'

Karl eventually settled down as a long-stay client of the Simon hostel, down the quays by the Liffey, among people who cared for him. His face aged beyond his years, his body become a little puffy. He never lost the quick laugh, the scorn for timidity or convention. He never lost his fondness for a quick hit from whatever he could shift from a chemist's shelves.

It was a damaged life, a limited one. He broke rules and laws, he was a serial offender, and no one suffered more for it than he did. The punishment far exceeded the crime. He never recovered from what was done to him in the early 1970s, when he fought back in the only way he could, by abusing his body, when they crammed the Serenace and the Mogadon and the Largactil into him until he lost the ability to walk. He remained damaged by the life he'd lived, but he survived too.

Sometimes he was okay when he was stoned or drunk, mostly when he was that way he was pitiable and sometimes frightening. When he was sober, he was funny, intelligent, interesting to be with. When you got to know this wasted, damaged individual just a little, he was far more than the sum of his crimes, far more than the sum of the things done to him. He was a nice man, a decent man.

He remained as much of the man he wanted to be as circumstances allowed. If those circumstances had been less savage, if his choices had not been so ruthlessly cut down, Karl might have become some of the things he had the capacity to be.

Karl struggled in his own desperate and self-destructive way. Others in similar circumstances find a less dangerous way of asserting themselves, some defer to overwhelming authority. Whatever gets you through.

Every time a compassionate judge demands that the State take seriously its responsibilities to endangered young people, or community workers despair as another social lifeboat is scuttled to save money for tax cuts, there are echoes of Karl's life, of the other Karls, of the Karls to be.

With his permission, I wrote about Karl in a book in the mid-1990s. There were times he threatened to sue me for that, make some easy money, then he'd laugh at the notion. He recommended the book to anyone who didn't believe his stories and, if they didn't believe he was in a book, he'd pop up to Eason's in O'Connell Street and steal them a copy. Startled at the thought he might end up in jail for stealing his own story, I pleaded with him not to do that again, and he laughed at my timidity.

Karl Crawley died in the summer of 1999. He was forty-seven.

Gene Kerrigan

A WOMAN BEFORE HER TIME

HANNIE LEAHY

My first memory of Olivia Hughes, affectionately know as Livie, was when, as a child, I was one of the many children, rich and poor, invited to the Christmas tree.

When she married, she moved away from Dublin to Annsgift, to a lovely old Georgian house in the heart of rural Ireland. She must have felt like an outsider, but quickly became involved in country life. She was a very handsome lady who showed no class distinction. She never looked down on anyone and spotted talent in everybody.

People looked forward to the Christmas tree for months ahead. It started with a party down in the flag-stone-floored kitchen in the cellar. The huge table was laid out with big plates of buttered barmbrack, home-made buns and all types of biscuits. Christmas crackers were strewn all over the table and every two pulled one between them. With the goodies on the table, we had home-made lemonade, and Livie always saw to it that any shy children got their share. This finished, we went up to the drawing room where the Christmas tree was beautifully decorated with tinsel and lots of presents. There was a present for each child, also a packet of sweets done up in green or red crepe paper, tied with either a silver or gold thread. Before we went home, we were taken to the pleasure ground where fireworks were set off. They went high up in the sky in many shapes and colours. They were the first ever seen in the area.

The threshing at Annsgift was also a great social event. It went on for three days. The helpers came from the neighbouring farms and were treated to a fine midday meal and afternoon tea. The quarter cask was also there for the thirsty workers. Livie worked all day in the kitchen to have everything right.

On the last evening, when the work was completed, the helpers and staff went home to wash and change and then came back for the threshing dance that went on until the small hours. Here, she was a great singer and her favourite songs were 'Way Down the Swanee River', 'Annie Laurie', 'Phil the Fluters Ball', when she made everyone join in. She got people out to dance who hadn't a step in their body.

Special places in her house included the flagstoned dairy where butter was made and eggs preserved for the Dublin market. Her store room contained shelves laden with jams, jellies, bottled fruit and chutneys to be shared or sold at the local market.

The orchards and gardens produced fruit, vegetables and flowers, gave food and shelter to the bees and, at times, my family's guinea pigs. All places were centres of learning, each plant explained, each birdsong identified and nothing wasted. I also remember the smell from the harness room, where hunting tackle was oiled and polished weekly.

She started a milk depot in Fethard and this was a blessing for the poorer people. She also organised a coffee van for the fair days. This was in the centre of the town and started operating early in the morning. The farmers and drovers out since the crack of dawn could buy tea, coffee or Bovril and either bread and butter or sandwiches. The staff were all volunteers and the biggest job they had was to extract the money from the farmers.

Livie introduced the Jubilee Nurse to Fethard and got volunteers once a year to visit every house in the parish to collect money to defray her expenses. She had the first ICA summer school started on the slopes of Slievenamon. She gathered together a group of women and among them some craft workers who taught lumra, rush work and different types of embroidery. They sang

and danced every night and brought in the local people
to join in the fun. They did Cashel sets, barn dances –
'Seige of Limerick', 'Waves of Tory' – and all kinds of
step dancing. They had plenty of musicians among them.
They used the water from the mountain streams for
cooking and also did some fishing. The summer school
and many more to follow were the forerunners of the
adult-education college at An Grianán, County Louth.

Livie was often seen cutting rushes in the River Suir.
When she had them ready, she got some of her staff to
come and collect them and spread them out in lofts to
dry. She went on to become the national president of
the ICA and Buan Cara. She never missed a monthly
meeting in Fethard and always made sure that there was
a social half-hour and also a nature competition. She
loved nature and knew the different bird sounds. She
knew the mushrooms that were safe to eat. I remember
her getting people to pick lots of primroses and make
bunches of them and send them by rail to the Adelaide
Hospital in Dublin for the patients.

With her friend Alice Armitage, she founded the
National Council for the Blind in Ireland. Her work in
South Tipperary went on for many years. She took off
on her High Nelly bicycle and often travelled thirty miles
in a day. The housebound people loved her and looked
forward to her visits. She taught Braille and bought an
accordion for an old neighbour who was visually im-
paired. She saw his talent.

Livie started a branch of Macra na Tuaithe in her
own house, where recycling was central to all activities.
Here she taught the children how to run a meeting and
how to prepare and enter for a show. She engendered
in them the concept that it wasn't all about winning and
yet they came out tops in many competitions. She drove
them to meetings and encouraged them to take part. As
a result of her involvement, she turned out some great

public speakers and many became well known in the community they worked in.

In 1947, she started the first country market in Ireland (Country Markets Ltd is a co-operative and there are now seventy markets nationwide). This she got going in the town hall in Fethard where it still is today. She worked tirelessly for weeks on end to get it going. She even went to England to find out how the Women's Institute ran theirs and decided to run hers on the same lines. She canvassed for a radius of twenty miles and roped in about forty members. She made a great success of it and got plenty of voluntary workers. I myself became the first treasurer and secretary and held the voluntary post for thirty-one years. I got help as to how the accounts should be kept from Mr Milner of the then Munster and Leinster Bank. I still take part every Friday and enjoy every minute of it.

The market ensured an outlet for surplus produce, especially eggs, which the local co-op could not handle and the hegglers had given up collecting. (People who collected eggs sometimes used them to barter for other produce.) It was difficult at first to get agreement to pay by cheque monthly. One penny commission was deducted from every shilling to defray running costs. The rent for the hall was five shillings a week. Suppliers found it hard to get used to writing out an invoice, which was very important as they had to collect unsold produce at the end. Some of the first customers remained with us until they died many years later. It was amazing that some of the women who got their first cheque came back and said it was the first time they had money of their own.

Friday was the chosen day and that was a good choice as it was the day pensioners were in town, and people were paying wages into the bank. It was also a fast day and eggs were used for dinner.

Livie was a great beekeeper and this meant we had plenty of honey. She loved her bees and couldn't understand anyone being afraid of them. She made some nice leaflets with pictures of fruit and flowers on them and had them distributed to all the houses in town before the opening day. Our motto was, and still is: 'The best at a fair price and money straight to the producers.'

She was a member of the Church of Ireland and her religion was very dear to her. She liked people to practise the religion to which they belonged. She was truly ecumenical and attended all church services. She played the organ in church and did the floral arrangements. The harvest thanksgiving was her highlight of the year. As well as church music, she played with the Clonmel Musical Society at their show every year. She took neighbours to see musicals that otherwise they would never see. Altogether, she was full of fun and could pick out grumpy people and called them poor old *angshores*.

She was also an artist, as was evident in her home, where a great variety of her talent was seen. One thing that never worried her was how she dressed. One day you could see her in a nice tweed suit but, more often than not, you could see her with her home-made canvas apron on.

In her latter years, she compiled a book on Fethard and its churches. She had a great love for old buildings, churches and castles, which she inherited from her mother. She liked telling young people about their history. She encouraged young people to learn local history and take an interest in the environment, renovating old buildings and cleaning old headstones.

Her one regret was that there weren't more women in politics as she thought they'd be better at running the country. In 1993, a plaque was erected in her memory outside the town hall where the first market took place.

The plaque was unveiled by President Mary Robinson and I presented a belt made by a market member to her. How proud she would have been to see our first woman president.

Livie inspired so many of us, and her vision continues to inspire people today as it lives on.

Hannie Leahy

WHO CARES?

GORDON LINNEY

When in disgrace with fortune and men's eyes
I all alone beweep my outcast state,
And trouble deaf heaven with my bootless cries,
And look upon myself, and curse my fate,
Wishing me like to one more rich in hope,
Featur'd like him, like him with friends possess'd.

W Shakespeare *'Sonnet 29'*

This is not a piece about anyone famous or anything like that. It is part of the stories of four people: an Aids victim, a homeless alcoholic, and an unmarried mother and her son. It is a tribute to people who knew the burden of social exclusion and condemnation. Their great achievement was that they worked so hard to retain their dignity while many around them compromised theirs.

It's easy to create, to invent *outsiders*. We do it all the time, making superficial judgements on people who cannot fit in or who are not allowed to fit in. Just take an individual or a group and attach a derogatory label of some kind and there you have it. Job done, a real genuine authentic outsider!

We describe refugees and asylum-seekers as scroungers with the subtext that they come to our country to take our houses, claim our welfare benefits and generally create a social mess.

This kind of labelling does several things. It puts space between 'them' and us and salves conscience. A scrounger does not deserve sympathy or compassion. It's a case of self-exclusion. It also suppresses discussion and avoids, for example, the possibility that we might be racist or selfish or dealing with awkward comparisons with the emigrating Irish, who, in their millions, left unemployment, poverty and disease, to make their way in Britain, America and elsewhere.

There are other labelled groups much like refugees: prisoners living 'in luxury with their colour televisions'; Travellers who are antisocial; 'winos' and other addicts who are classed as dropouts; Aids victims who had to be immoral according to a certain type of moral extremist and were being punished for their sins. Even God is drawn into the labelling game! Richard Holloway, one-time Bishop of Edinburgh, was very critical of that kind of moral confusion and accused those who saw Aids as a divine punishment of representing God as a kind of urban terrorist indiscriminately tossing bombs into a crowded street.

I have a scene of total isolation engraved in my memory. I was visiting a church-run hospital in southwest Uganda with which my parish has strong links and was invited to join an Aids counselling and support team visiting a village several miles away. In one of those thatched African huts in a banana plantation, I saw this poor woman, lying on a straw mat, alone, dying. Her husband had contracted Aids and, having infected her, died some time previously. When she became ill, her children were taken from her and, according to local custom, placed many miles away with the father's family. This woman who had lost her husband and her children would soon lose her life, yet somehow she retained her dignity and spoke lovingly and without resentment about her husband and her children. She was an outsider because people were afraid of infection and some would have moral reservations about her situation.

In reality, she was an innocent victim who had lost everything and who was now facing a death sentence. I had a feeling of utter helplessness and not a little anger at the injustice of it all. It certainly brought home the terrible injustice of a business world, which had the medical means to help but refused to do so in this case because the country could not afford to pay the going rate for drugs.

There is another side to this process of exclusion. We don't just cut others off from our world without effect. We detach ourselves from one of the better characteristics of our own humanity. We suppress what is almost certainly a natural disposition to have pity, to show compassion. We become less human. Just as John Donne recognised that 'any man's death diminishes me' so, too, we need to be aware that anyone's exclusion or marginalisation diminishes all of us.

Jim was a homeless 'wino' who hung out around the Liberties of Dublin in my days in Donore Avenue. He was a regular caller to our home and often entertained our children. In harsh weather, he would turn up with one of his buddies and ask for a voucher for the Iveagh Hotel – the hostel – but, as often as not, he would only want some water or occasionally a sandwich. One day I met him in a small side street and, as we chatted, a woman came out of a house and chased the two of us with a sweeping brush, calling him all sorts of names and telling me, collar and all, that I should have more sense than to be mixing with 'the likes of him'.

However, the purpose of reciting this incident is not to criticise her, but to admit a personal failing. One Sunday afternoon I was in St Patrick's Cathedral lined up with the other clergy and ready to process behind the choir for Evensong. I felt a tug on my sleeve just as we were about to move off. It was Jim wanting me for something. By now the procession was on its way and me with it. Jim was left behind as I advanced up the long aisle to keep my appointment with God in the beautiful language of the Book of Common Prayer.

One of the readings that same afternoon told us where Jesus would be found, in the least of these his brethren. I suddenly remembered Jim. I had left the real Jesus behind at the other end of the great church in the touch of an outsider. I never did discover what was required of me that day – an opportunity had been lost for ever.

I am often reminded of the way in which social and religious conventions combine to exclude and create situations that do terrible damage to people. Mary was a seventeen-year-old country girl who got pregnant. Her father, a proud and strict man, ordered that a suitcase be packed and she was ordered to leave and never come back. She had disgraced the family. Homeless, she turned to a local cleric who arranged temporary care and eventually she was placed in a home for unmarried mothers-to-be, an outcast. It is almost impossible to imagine the pain and grief of that whole family but, most of all, the girl herself. When her baby, Tom, was born, she went out to work but visited him every weekend for several years at the foster parents' home. One day, she called as usual to be told he had gone away. She would never see him alive again. In time she married and had other children.

Many years later, she was contacted to be told that her son had died. She immediately thought of one of the children from her marriage but discovered that it was her long-lost first-born, Tom. He had lived a very uncertain life and would have been seen by many as a dropout. Somehow he had tracked his mother down but never contacted her. Among his paltry possessions, photos of her were found, taken at a distance, and notes about her husband and other children. These enabled the authorities to make the link with his mother when he died. It seemed he almost stalked her but he never had the courage to approach her for he was the complete outsider. Little did he know how welcome he would have been.

This story is a dossier of the injustices heaped upon a group of people by something we like to call 'society'. The young girl kicked out of her home, the child taken and in time kept from his mother, the young man isolated from his siblings and forced to wander among strangers. An outsider yes, but totally innocent too. In a very special way, Tom is the man to caution us in our attitude to the stranger among us, the outsider. When we encounter the Toms of this world, the one thing we can be certain of is that our perception of his circumstances will be completely wide of the mark.

Jean Vanier, founder of L'Arche Communities has powerful insights into the mind of the excluded and rejected and he gives this advice in his book *The Broken Body*:

> Do not be surprised at rejection by broken people. They have suffered a great deal at the hands of the knowledgeable and the powerful – doctors, psychologists, sociologists, social workers, politicians, the police and others. They have suffered so much from broken promises, from people wanting to learn from experiments or to write a thesis and then having gained what they wanted – votes, recognition, an impressive book or article – going away and never coming back.
>
> Rejected people are sick and tired of 'good' and 'generous' people, of people who claim to be Christians, of people who come to them on their pedestals of pride and power to do them good.

No wonder their hearts are closed to new people. They are waiting for someone who really cares and who sees in them the light of love and wisdom, who recognises their gifts and their beauty; someone who will accept them just as they are with no preconceived ideas that they should change.

Gordon Linney

OUTSIDE THE CIRCLE

RAY LYNOTT

He was convinced the leak had a life of its own. Drip, drip, echoing in the aluminium bucket at his feet, relentless like pain. The circular stain on the bay-window ceiling, darker at the edges, had widened after another attempt at repair. God or the devil alone knew where it came from; laws and logic were different there.

He didn't say this to his wife standing beside him.

Once before they had been fatalistic, with dire consequences. Why should he remember now? Policeman at the door. Child dead.

Then there were other bottomless dimensions of horror, loss, inadequacy; fatalism might have been allowed, so they assumed, until it was obvious that disaster was compounded by the simple act of looking at each other, eye to eye, and saying, 'We feared something like this might happen, didn't we? We were powerless.' His own ordinary voice, that time in the cold kitchen. Timid Ann agreeing by a quick nod of her head. In the silence that followed, they both knew: they were betraying the child's whole existence, demolishing her. The ultimate treason.

Of course, they tried to retract. Ann tried. Ineffectual, as always. 'No, we're not being fair to her, to ourselv…' She didn't finish the word. And then he was the one who nodded. Too late.

They began to blame the child's grandmother. He did. 'Sending the child so often to stay with an old woman in remote Donegal, what did we expect?'

Old woman: his own mother. The way he always thought of… seanBhríd Nic Shuibhne. Even as a child, hearing Kildea, her so-called friend, talking about her to the postmistress: the fact that Bríd wouldn't have a phone installed, that she wouldn't use her widow's insurance money to buy a car and learn to drive, that she was so old fashioned and religious, yet she had a row with the parish priest and wouldn't go to church. '*Seanbhean dheileoir*,' Kildea said, thinking his archaic description of her as cold and morose wouldn't be understood.

The old woman was always cold, inward looking. And a snob. Cruel downturn of the grey lips when she asked if he couldn't do better than marry into a family of 'tattie hokers'. He and Ann moved to Dublin.

Yet the child loved her. Their bright, red-haired daughter and the old woman always got on. It was a mystery to himself, as it was to his wife, he supposed.

Sheila was a strange, pretty child. She would turn into a beautiful assured woman, different to her mother or her grandmother. She was already showing all the signs.

And then she died. Suddenly, on holidays with the old woman, just after her thirteenth birthday. Without warning, of any kind. Heart failure, the report said: undetected abnormality... the words handing out blame. And there was the other cant; it wouldn't bring the child back, he said to Ann. They didn't need to know. There wouldn't be any more.

'*Tachrán girsí*,' the grandmother repeated, dry-eyed, rocking herself in a chair by the fire. Her grief, if that's what it was, took the form of describing the girl, endlessly. 'Hair as red as the setting sun this time of year.' She spoke in the Irish-English concoction that was her own, private, bookish, leftover from her teaching days. '*Lán de chroí 's de aigneadh, lán de sprid*, brim full, my Sheileen, wee seal of life itself, *mo róinín*.'

He knew his mother's ways too well, her stories of seals and seal children. She buried the sadness of her life in stories that she told again and again to the infinite boredom of all around her, except the girl.

She refused the phone and television because they

would interfere with her stories and her 'folk', by which she meant the characters of these stories. Hers was the last of the *céilí* houses; but the cronies who gathered round her were a narrowing circle, as much afraid as fond of her and her busy tongue. Sheila alone never seemed to get bored with the *ráiméis* or the ways of the small, old-fashioned granny who had let herself become more and more a creature out of her own imagination. The growing girl would throw her arms protectively around the bent, frail figure, especially when it was obvious that her father was about to lose patience with his mother.

And then word came, through the police, that the girl was dead. He had left her in Rannafast only a week before. The old woman had been particularly needful in letters, day after day. And even though Sheila had already spent most of July with her, the granny was asking her to celebrate her birthday there, on the first of August, and to stay until after Mary's Day on the 15th.

He knew 15th August was particularly difficult for his mother: the day his father and two brothers were officially declared dead, years after their boat disappeared off Seal Rock, the years of the old woman's perpetual coiling croon, 'They return from the sea, but not from the grave, they return from…'

That August was Sheila's first birthday following her quiet early-summer transition to womanhood; and both he and Ann wanted to make some kind of an occasion out of it. He knew that. Ann wouldn't talk about such matters, but he knew. Obviously, Sheila felt differently. And his mother had the final say, as she always had.

The funeral was a farce, because of the old woman's antics. She wouldn't believe the girl was dead. And yet she insisted on a Donegal burial, in the already crowded grave. It seemed as if she was taking delight in parting the wound that would never heal.

And then, traipsing them all down to the cold, wind-swept beach. The weather was unseasonable. The Atlantic like a pack of wild, vicious curs, wirey-grey, frothing at the mouth and snapping at their feet. The boat that never came up again must have been dragged under by such viciousness, or worse. Beloved giants of men…

Relentless knife-stroke, instantly transformed; the numbness now damp, raw cold blowing in his face as he saw his mother tugging Kildea's arm, telling him to draw a circle on the wet sand with his stick.

She stepped inside the circle. Kildea, regressive as she, at the edge of the circle encouraging her to begin the Hail Mary. Her strong teacher's voice, 'Hail Mary, full of grace…', then the tight, weathered face opening up, long, grey wisps of her hair blowing back in the rough wind. The intent gaze moving to an empty space to the right of Kildea, and the needle-sharp eyes indicating that the old woman saw something, or thought she saw something there.

'*Gabh isteach chugam, a leanbh.*'

Talking to the dead girl, asking her into the circle! He was frozen to the spot. Ann clutching his arm. The parish of old people, like grey stone statues, behind them. He remembered the cold, more than the sequence of events. His mother's screech. But exactly what happened before she fell senseless with that unearthly sound, he wasn't sure. Kildea telling them to look round, that there was a seal making for the sea. All he and Ann saw, or so Ann agreed afterwards, was the wind shifting long, brown streamers of shining seaweed out of reach of the vicious, grey, frothing August tide.

They drove back to Dublin in silence, leaving the old woman in Letterkenny Hospital.

Now, a year later, his mother was in the new plot beside the old grave, on her own; and such a ridiculous

nuisance as a leak over the bay window was haunting
their red-brick house here in the heart of Dublin city,
taking over the remains of their lives.

In the cold front room, he and Ann were cradling
coffee cups in their hands, silently looking up at the damp
circle that was spreading on the ceiling, after the builder
had promised an end to the problem. It had a life of its
own, this leak. There were such things as household gods
and demons. Beside them, one had no chance, was a
stranger. But he couldn't say that to Ann at this moment, or ever. She would think he was becoming his
mother, even if she wouldn't have the courage to put it
in such words.

And what... if one day she did have courage... finally? He looked at her; she was looking straight back at
him, out of a circle spreading.

In 1960, when I did my Leaving Certificate, Seosamh
Mac Grianna's strange collection of stories *An Grá Agus
An Ghruaim* was on the Irish syllabus, along with *An
Baile Seo 'Gainne* by 'an Seabhac' (1913). These were the
only complete works of twentieth-century fiction we
read in a secondary school (St Patrick's College, Cavan)
where classical rather than modern languages were taught
(saying which, by the way, is not a complaint).

On the English syllabus then, we only had prose ex-
tracts, mostly essays, and one of Shakespeare's plays.
So, the Mac Grianna made an impression on me because it was a small but complete body of work that
obviously came from a wonderfully active, if slightly
cranky, tradition-fed, musical and poetic mind. And even
though it was first published in 1929, well before I was
born, I could respond to these stories about lives and

loves lost to 'the other world', to sickness, to famine (the Famine), to miserliness, greed and pride. Mac Grianna's world fixed itself in that part of the imagination all good fiction reaches.

Last year when, once again, I came across the slim blue book with its *cló gaelach* (as originally published by Brún agus Ó Nualláin), I was delighted; and, after I reread the first story 'Bíonn Súil Le Muir Ach Ní Bhíonn Súil Le hUaigh' ('There's Return from the Sea but there's No Return from the Grave'), I wrote 'Outside the Circle'. My tale is not a translation, and I wouldn't even call it a version because I haven't tried to keep to the purpose, to encompass the mood or match the resounding language of Mac Grianna's story. But some kind of osmosis happened while I was writing it. I have to admit, I was also going through a house renovation at the time, and beginning to believe my own theory about the autonomous life of leaks. And then I saw an RTÉ television documentary that made me curious about Seosamh Mac Grianna's anguished life.

He was born in Rannafast in 1901. There were eleven in his family: storytellers, songwriters and an older brother, Séamus, who published under the pseudonym Máire.

Later, these two brothers quarrelled so vehemently that Seosamh changed his family name from the 'O Grianna' his brother used, to 'Mac Grianna'; that was while both of them worked for years in Dublin as translators for the government-funded Irish-language publishing house, An Gúm. This was tedious work Seosamh took on because he wasn't allowed to teach full time after he had been interned during the Civil War as a member of the IRA. He had qualified from St Patrick's Teacher Training College in Dublin in 1921 and, subsequently, did some temporary teaching but, by the early

1930s when he needed a permanent job, he had to turn to An Gúm where he worked from 1933 to 1953, hobbled within landscapes created by Walter Scott, Emily Brontë, Joseph Conrad and others.

One of his own best works was rejected by An Gúm in 1935: *An Druma Mór*, about Orangemen and Nationalists sharing a marching drum in a Donegal parish. It wasn't published until 1969, by which time Mac Grianna was the worse for a nervous disorder born out of loneliness and hardship that had dogged him for most of his life. He spent his last Dublin days in a gatehouse near Dollymount. But he had travelled abroad when he could. *An Bhreatain Bheag* (1937) *Na Lochlannaigh* (1938) and *Mo Bhealach Féin* (1940) are at once books of travel and autobiography.

Seosamh Mac Grianna died in Letterkenny Mental Hospital in 1990.

Towards the end of *Mo Bhealach Féin* (*My Own Path*) he says:

> My journey was done. I was proud of it. If anyone asked what was the point of my travels, I'd have a job answering them except to say that it was my way of doing things…
>
> Life is above and beyond the small shelter of words we put over it. Not everything can be explained. We're like blind people trying to help each other along, with whatever experience and advice is available to us.

Ray Lynott

OWEN SHEEHY SKEFFINGTON: READER IN FRENCH, TCD

DAVID MCCONNELL

Owen Sheehy Skeffington, a bespectacled, upright, stolid figure, wearing his black gown, walked into the large, tiered, black-wooded and uncomfortable Victorian lecture theatre in the Museum Building one day in early 1963. His head tilted slightly as he looked at the serried ranks, some mischief in his eye as he thought how best to influence this unpromising lot.

Most of us were honours students of science or medicine or engineering. We were required to take a pass arts course, in principle to broaden our minds, and in fact to justify the receipt of the degree Bachelor of Arts, which we would receive if all went well, in four to seven years time – even scientists, doctors and engineers at Trinity receive a BA on graduation. Few of us had more than a passing interest in French.

To those who did not know of Skeffington, the prospects for the course were not great. We *had* to attend his lectures, we *had* to pass the examination in French, and we *had* to wear gowns – unheard of in science. He could not have looked more of an establishment figure, acting for the establishment. The truth was quite different – he had been an outsider all his life. Appropriately, he was to lecture us brilliantly and wittily on *L'Étranger* by Camus, published not long before in 1955. In my four years of college, he was the only person to lecture me on matters of general social or political interest – he taught us about France in a way that I still appreciate.

He was known as Skeff to the students and graduates, and he was a hero to many, one of the few public voices of reason on the bleak, featureless, yet disturbing social landscape of the 1950s and early 1960s.

His story has been beautifully told by his wife Andrée

(*Skeff: A life of Owen Sheehy Skeffington 1909–1970* Lilliput
Press, 1991), and I encourage all to read this extraordinary book.

He was born into a highly educated, political family.
His parents, Francis (Frank) Skeffington and Hanna
Sheehy, both university graduates, took each other's surname and, as one, they became even more intensely involved in all sorts of radical activities, but not usually of
the sort for which the period is remembered in modern
Ireland. They were nationalists (in an international sort
of way), but also pacifists and feminists, humanists, advanced in their ideas about education and the family,
opponents of conscription, and propagandists for reason, common sense, fairness, social justice and simple
decency. Frank, a graduate of the Jesuit University College Dublin, where he had thrived in the company of a
remarkable group of students and staff, had been Registrar of the college for a few years.

He lectured and wrote, making a living from freelance journalism, even travelling on a lecture tour of
the United States. On the Tuesday of Easter Week 1916,
Frank had been trying to prevent the looting that accompanied the Rising. While walking home, he had been
arrested and imprisoned with two other journalists by a
Captain Colthurst – the next day all were shot in Porto-
bello Barracks, Rathmines, without trial. Colthurst, seeking evidence to justify the murderous executions, raided
the family home on the Friday. Owen, aged seven, described the raid in his diary.

Subsequently, a court martial found Colthurst guilty
but insane, and a public inquiry followed, but neither
satisfied Hanna's quest for justice. She turned down an
offer of £10,000 from Asquith to stop her campaign
and then, avoiding the police, travelled with Owen on
forged passports to New York to pursue her campaign
against the British government. Hanna, daughter of

David Sheehy MP and a sister in law of Francis Cruise
O'Brien and Tom Kettle, was to become the main influence on her only child Owen.

Hanna and Owen returned to Ireland in 1918. In
1920, aged eleven, he went to the non-sectarian Earlsfort
House School in Adelaide Road and came under the
influence of the joint headmaster Mr Alfred Le Peton,
an Englishman whose father was French. This was the
same year that Samuel Beckett moved from Earlsfort
House to Portora School, Enniskillen. Anthony Cronin
doubts that Le Peton inspired a love of France in anyone, but both Samuel Beckett and Owen Sheehy Skeffington were Le Peton's students at a most formative time
of their lives and this suggests otherwise. Andrée Sheehy
Skeffington attests to the sense of 'equality and tolerance throughout' the school which stemmed from 'Lep'.
(See also *The Life of Samuel Beckett* by James Knowlson,
Bloomsbury Press, 1966).

In 1922, Le Peton set up a new school, Sandford Park
School (SPS), in Ranelagh, bringing fifty students from
Earlsfort House, including Owen. Though the predomi-
nant attitude would have been that of diffident unionism, and Owen was always keen to express his own by
now independent and different views, he thrived at
Sandford Park, becoming head boy in 1926, the year in
which he captained SPS to win the Leinster Schools
Senior Cricket Cup.

This was also the year his cousin, Conor Cruise
O'Brien, was entered in the school by his recently wid-
owed mother. Conor's enrolment in SPS encountered
huge opposition from the Catholic authorities (see
Memoir: My Life and Themes by Conor Cruise O'Brien,
Poolbeg Press, 1998). The problem was simple: Sandford
Park School was not a Catholic school, and not considered suitable by the Church for the education of Catholic boys. Moreover, the school was exceptional in the

diversity of its students and its commitment to what is now called multiculturalism: one third of the boys were nominally Protestant, one third Catholic and one third Jewish. Owen and Conor came as outsiders amongst outsiders, and were accepted. Andrée comments that: 'Owen's seven schools were characterised by a degree of freedom from orthodoxy, and a climate of friendship, co-operation and trust.'

In 1927, Owen won an entrance scholarship to Trinity College, choosing Trinity he said impishly because, 'I could continue to play cricket there.' It was a bigger test than Sandford Park, for unionism meant a great deal more in Trinity. The college was still largely the preserve of the recently dispossessed establishment, and strongly Anglican. Front Square was dominated by the Church of Ireland chapel, and no Provost had ever been appointed who was a Presbyterian, Methodist or Quaker, much less a Catholic, Jew or agnostic. But it was a tolerant place, and it valued intelligence, wit and sporting ability, probably in equal measure, qualities finding full expression in Owen. But Trinity was disconnected from the republicans, Catholics and Irish revivalists who were now running the country, and who had taken control of the National University of Ireland.

At Trinity, Owen, who was a strong nationalist and agnostic, was once again an outsider who thrived among outsiders. He won a Foundation Scholarship in English and French in his second year, giving him the privilege of free rooms and Commons (evening meal) in college, he fought for the rights of women in college, he debated in the College Historical Society ('The Hist'), which adored him till the end, he boxed and played cricket, and he sat if the band played 'God Save the King'. Beckett taught him and, after graduating in 1931 with a First Class degree, Owen followed Beckett to Paris as *lecteur* in the prestigious École Normale Supérieure.

Skeffington was appointed to a lectureship in Trinity in 1936, once again following Beckett.

For the next quarter of a century, Dr Owen Sheehy Skeffington devoted himself to teaching and politics, 'sacrificing his scholarly to his political interests'. He receives only slight mention in the major histories of Trinity College because his main interests lay outside its walls. There is no doubt that he had a fine mind and was capable of outstanding scholarship, but he was much more the socially engaged man of action. He was a dedicated and much admired teacher, a meticulous and original lecturer, and the students of the college called on him time and again to speak at their meetings, including many inaugurals of the Hist. He became involved in many political societies, promoting social justice, secularism and so forth.

He was a socialist, and had become a member of the Labour Party in 1934. But, he was 'too independent for any party to harbour him'. He had become a university person, accustomed to somewhat more rational, incisive and tolerant debate, to the extent that he often taxed the generosity of his colleagues in Trinity. The Labour Party could not accept that he was entitled to criticise the leadership and expelled him in miserable circumstances in 1943. From then on, only Trinity could hold him.

I remember my first sightings of Owen Sheehy Skeffington. He had become a governor of Sandford Park School and, in 1953, he participated with six other old boys and one parent, to form a new board and rescue the school from closure. I entered Sandford in 1955 and was puzzled by the occasional appearance at the school of someone who seemed to be an inspector but clearly was not. He rode a bicycle, he usually wore a light mackintosh, a suit and a Trinity tie. He sometimes attended cricket and hockey cup matches, he ate lunch with the boys from time to time and, most remarkably, he would attend the occasional class, sitting at the back.

At my first prize giving, he sat on the stage with the other governors and gradually all fell into place. This was Dr Skeffington, Chairman of the Education Committee of the Board, who liked to see for himself that all was as it should be. I never heard that any teacher objected but, thirty years later, I did not dare to emulate him. The boys came to know him and to respect him as much as the teachers. By this time, he had become one of the most-powerful critics in Irish politics, feared and hated by many, but admired by those who wanted a liberal and open Ireland.

One afternoon in about 1956, he came to the school to found the SPS Debating Society. I can see him still, in the classroom of Upper IV, telling us that speeches should be carefully prepared, that they should be reduced to notes on postcards, that the notes should be used as aids to keep the speech on track, perhaps with key phrases fully written out for use in making strong points, and that we should 'stand up, speak up and shut up'. He noted that wit was one of the strongest weapons in debate. He asked us never to be discourteous, and always to be in control of our own ideas. His Sandford Park was to be dedicated to the development of free, informed and independent minds. That debating society still exists and recently won the *Observer* Mace for British and Irish schools.

Dr Skeffington had arranged for Trevor Dagg, his former student in Trinity, to become the new headmaster of Sandford Park in 1954. Dagg was a truly great headmaster and the style and quality of the modern school owe more to him than to anyone else. Like Skeffington, Dagg was a humanist, a socialist, a reader of the Manchester *Guardian* and a francophile. The school, as in 1922, was one third Jewish, but had only one Catholic boy. The hierarchical ban on Catholics attending non-Catholic schools had worked – Ireland had become steadily and sadly more narrow-minded in the first thirty years of independence.

The school itself had a few more steps to take in the transition from multi-denominational to non-denominational, and Trevor and Owen conspired with glee. At morning assembly, the headmaster had customarily read the Church of Ireland prayer for the day (the collect), and I believe we said the Lord's Prayer. After the Christian prayers, the Jews came in, and Owen's elder son, Francis. Francis puzzled me; I knew he was not Catholic and I had never heard of humanists. Then, at the beginning of a new year, the collect and the Lord's Prayer were replaced by a gentle invocation to think of others and do good – religion had been taken out by Owen and Trevor. From then on, the Jews and agnostics had to be in school by 9 o'clock sharp like the rest of us.

The 1950s were somewhat unsettling for those of us who were outsiders. While we were not threatened, neither did we feel welcomed. We moved in our non-Catholic archipelago; Jews, Protestants and agnostics, isolated to varying extents in our own schools, golf, rugby and tennis clubs, churches and synagogues, scouts and guides, even banks, breweries and insurance companies. In the cities, where we were grouped in certain neighbourhoods, we were comfortable enough until we fell in love with a Catholic, or out of love, where religious affiliation or disaffiliation did not count one way or the other.

Archbishop McQuaid was the figure who seemed most intent on getting us to sign up or leave the country, applying *ne temere* with enthusiasm and, unwisely from his point of view, leaving Trinity College to us. Dr McQuaid helped to make sure that divorce and contraception were proscribed by the 1937 Constitution, not worrying about homosexuality, which was unimaginable.

The Irish Times was our newspaper and Trinity was our bastion; within Trinity and *The Irish Times*, Skeffington, the socialist and humanist, was the somewhat unlikely champion of conventionally religious, middle-class Protestant and Jewish businessmen, professional men and academics. He took on Dr McQuaid and his allies in a remarkable series of controversies at meetings and often amplified through letters to *The Irish Times*. His reputation for persuading perceptive minds grew ever stronger – in 1949 he was excluded from speaking at the Literary and Historical Society in UCD by the McQuaid ally and President of UCD, Dr Michael Tierney. The motion was 'That the ideals of the Communist Manifesto are worthy of humanity'. The whole meeting was, in fact, cancelled by the college.

In 1954, the outsider was elected to one of the Trinity seats in the Seanad, the only way in which he or anyone remotely like him was likely to be elected to the Oireachtas at that time.

Paul Blanshard, an American, published *The Irish and Catholic Power* in 1953 (Beacon Press, Boston). It is a powerful analysis of the position of the Catholic Church in Ireland. Skeffington appears, for example in the so-called Papal Nuncio Incident. This took place at a meeting of the International Affairs Association of Ireland in 1952 at which an address concerning the differences between the communist government and the Catholic Church was delivered. It was called 'Yugoslavia: The Pattern of Persecution'. When the address had ended, the chairman ruled, contrary to normal practice, that there could be no questions or comments. Skeffington objected and the ruling of the chair was overturned by a vote. His friend Hubert Butler, an expert on the history and politics of Yugoslavia, then presented the 'non-Catholic side to the Yugoslav story' and compared the regime of the Croatian Fuehrer, Anet Pavelitch, with the sort of regime sought for Ireland by the reactionary organisation Maria Duce. This caused the Papal Nuncio to walk out, and a heated correspondence developed in the press.

As a side effect, Hubert Butler was forced to resign from the Kilkenny Archaeological Society. And an invitation to Skeffington to speak at the student debating society at the Rathmines Technical College was withdrawn, apparently on the instructions of the Vocational Education Committee, and much to the embarrassment of the students.

Irish society in those days could, and did, turn in miserly ways on those who dared to question the Catholic Church; almost no one stood up for either Skeffington or Butler. I found a second-hand copy of Blanshard, a gift from Skeffington to one S. S. (probably Séamus Scully, one of his many argumentative friends) with a note inscribed: 'A great book! And will do Séamus a power of good!' Many years later, Catholics and non-Catholics alike, we have cause to think more deeply about the matters signalled so clearly by Blanshard, Skeffington, Butler and a very few others in the 1950s and early 1960s.

Skeffington was a great parliamentarian in the sense that he was an inveterate and eloquent opponent of the government, all governments of the day – none of them could measure up to his standards or match his persistence. He spoke and wrote as the champion of minorities and the poor, opposing extremes such as capital and corporal punishment, and apartheid, seeking rapprochement with the unionists in Ulster, urging the government to provide good and free meals in schools – few sensible social or political projects escaped his support, and humbug invited his finely aimed barbs. He demolished an insufferable born-again Christian, Malcolm

Muggeridge, in a famous joust in the Mansion House, ending his speech with the suggestion that 'Jesus wept'.

I am not sure that Skeffington has been fully recognised for his contributions to modern Ireland, and I think especially of his influence on the students of the 1960s who later did so much to change Ireland in the 1970s and 1980s. Two biographies of Mary Robinson are to hand, but neither investigates the influence that I suspect he had on her. As a student, she could not have avoided his influence in Trinity in the 1960s. After she graduated she joined the Labour Party, perhaps seeing it as he did in the 1930s, as the only possible refuge for a liberal. Then she joined him as a Trinity Senator after the election of 1969.

But they had only a short time together in Leinster House. His health had not been strong for many years and he died aged sixty-one, too young, in 1970. At his funeral, Seán Ó Faoláin concluded that he was 'one of the noblest and most complete men our country has ever produced – the inspiration and, very often, the conscience of all who knew him'.

I will close with this typically honest comment by Garret FitzGerald in his autobiography (*All in a Life. Garret FitzGerald: An autobiography* Gill and Macmillan, 1991). In 1949, FitzGerald thought and wrote that Skeffington was a Communist, and found himself in receipt of solicitor's letters. To this day, FitzGerald cannot imagine what came over him, but I wonder is he being fair to himself. Like many young men in the 1940s, graduating after the end of a terrible war, when 'an iron curtain [had] descended across the continent', FitzGerald must have been concerned about communism, and many others were lining up against Skeffington. Like them, FitzGerald just got the wrong end of the Skeffington stick. In any case, he has made amends by one of the

most apposite comments about Skeff. 'Although avow-
edly agnostic, his behaviour was of the kind commonly
called Christian, although not universal amongst people
of that faith.'

David McConnell

A HOME FOR SEAN

MAMO MCDONALD

A wise mother, when asked which of her children she loved the most, replied 'the one who is sick until they are better and the one who is far from home until they return'.

When I think of Cathleen O'Neill, I think of a warrior queen, strong, intrepid and brave. An activist 'by blood and conviction', Cathleen has espoused many causes, most notable being her indication of the rights of women, deprived of educational opportunities in early life, to have a second chance. As a young mother, she joined Kilbarrack Local Education for Adult Renewal (KLEAR) where her small children would be cared for while she studied. Progressing through the system, Cathleen eventually became the director of KLEAR and went on to graduate with a Masters degree in Equality Studies from University College Dublin. Now Cathleen heads up Saol, another innovative project aimed at helping women drug users recover and develop through education.

Above all else though, Cathleen O'Neill is a passionate mother. She has been the sole parent of her five children ever since her twins were babies. When Cathleen talks about her children, all now adults, her love, concern and pride shines through – never more so than when she speaks of Sean, now twenty-two, who has to be the main focus for her care and love.

Sean and his twin sister Roisín were born prematurely, seven weeks early. When he was three, Sean was diagnosed with a moderate mental handicap and also displayed signs of autism, which was confirmed when he was six years old. Living at home, Sean attended St Michael's House on a daily basis, but became hard to manage when he became completely hyperactive and started to run away frequently.

When, through exhaustion and stress, Cathleen had a nervous breakdown, a residential placement for Sean became a matter of urgency. No suitable place was available in the Republic, so he was sent northwards and, for the next ten years, Sean's term-time home was at the Camphill Community in Hollywood, County Down. Difficulties in adapting to change made it hard for him to settle, but he did so eventually, helped by the loving care he received and the fortnightly visits of his mother, who travelled from Dublin to reassure him and maintain family links. Sean also came home for holidays at Christmas, Easter and summertime. During these holidays, Cathleen remembers, she would sometimes walk with him seven or eight miles a day to use up some of Sean's boundless energy, so helping him sleep at night.

As the end of his placement at Camphill approached, Cathleen began the tortuous task of finding a home suitable for Sean's needs and capabilities. In 1997, two years before his time in the Camphill centre ended, Cathleen wrote to the official in charge of the services within the Eastern Regional Health Authority.

> He [Sean] is extremely active, extremely vocal and extremely difficult but also very beautiful… He is six foot two and is no longer able to manage the structure and routine of the school situation. The Camphill Community has been vital in his life for the past seven years but we are now in a very different situation with Sean. He needs far too much care and Camphill can no longer provide that comprehensive service. Anyhow, it is no longer education we are talking about, we are now talking about his survival. I acknowledge the huge debt I

owe them. They have been incredible about Sean and the difficulties he posed them.

Please get in touch with me soon about a place for Sean. All of the family are very concerned.

Three years later not much had changed. Cathleen was still writing letters and making representations on behalf of Sean. Determined that he would not be condemned to life in a psychiatric hospital, she explored every possibility. Hearing that the Irish Society for Autism (ISA) was establishing a care facility at Kinnegad, County Westmeath, Cathleen applied for a place for Sean. There then followed a lengthy process of evaluation, assessment and case consultations. The slow progress necessitated a request for a six-month extension to Sean's placement at Camphill.

When a place was offered by ISA in the spring of 2000, Cathleen was told it would be available in a matter of weeks, as soon as the new staff were on board, so one can imagine her surprise and shock when she received a letter stating that Sean's placement had been changed to Dunfirth (another facility in Westmeath).

After a silence of some weeks, there was even worse news, not from ISA, but from a health board official who told Cathleen the offer of a place for Sean had been withdrawn. Her calls to ISA were not returned and her letters received no reply. With no prospect of a placement, Sean returned from Camphill to Cathleen's care.

When a place was offered by the health board, it was in St Ita's, Portrane. Cathleen and her entire family went to see it and afterwards sat outside in the car weeping that Sean should now be condemned to a locked ward in a psychiatric hospital. Then Cathleen galvanised all her resources and a radical plan of action was put in place. She rallied friends, neighbours and other mothers of children with autism. She made contact by email, phone and word of mouth, she alerted the media to focus national television, radio and newspaper coverage.

On the 15th August 2000, a group gathered on the lawn outside the offices of the Eastern Regional Health Authority (ERHA) at Dr Steevens' Hospital. The women set up camp, displayed placards and engaged with the media, handing out press releases and conducting interviews. Striking images appeared nationwide on television and newspapers.

Led by Cathleen O'Neill, the group demanded a suitable placement for Sean, an end to the practice of accommodating people with intellectual disabilities in psychiatric institutions and the setting up of an inter-departmental group to examine ways to deal with the shortfall in services for these voiceless members of our society (3,500 autism sufferers without appropriate services).

Health board personnel included many who were sympathetic to the cause and offers of toilet and tea-making services were given to the protestors. During the two-night camp-out, a tentative offer of a place for Sean was made and he, subsequently, went to a care facility in Ashford, County Wicklow, where he is happy and well cared for. Cathleen's visits to be with him continue and holidays are still spent at home. Always on call when the need arises, Cathleen says:

> Every penny I've earned has been put into securing Sean's place in a society that offers him so little, mediating with him and for him. Now I am nearing retirement without any resources left, I worry more for him though. Sean's care is high cost and he is in constant danger of being a victim of

cutbacks. St Ita's in Portrane will always be in the picture as it is a cheap option. Now I am older and tireder and it gets harder.

Still, I wouldn't count Cathleen out yet. The light of battle still shines in her eyes.

Mamo McDonald

MAD OUT OF IT

CHRISTY MOORE

When Alice called me about this project, the first outsider I thought of was Vic Rose in the last race at a Curragh race meeting in 1958. I was thirteen years old and put my last shilling on her at 33/1 and she cantered home. What a time we had, me and Joe Coffey. But this is probably not the sort of outsider Alice has in mind.

I don't rightly know who the insiders are. Take our highest-profile multimillionaires – are they the ultimate insiders? Does sitting atop a baked-bean mountain or a cardboard-box empire constitute the inside? I don't think so. Taoiseach, Tánaiste, Minister – is this the inside?

Life with little truth, photocall, soundbite, sexy headline, sounds like the inside of a mad house, power monopoly and trivial pursuits: 'In the know', 'Mad out of it', 'She got outside herself', 'Out of my head', 'Get out of it'.

On Sunday 16th March 2003, Rachel Corrie was mangled to death by an Israeli bulldozer on the Gaza strip, an American outsider inside the hearts of Palestinian children. This morning, our Taoiseach and Tánaiste are insiders within Dubya's world regime, but they are outsiders as the terror rains down, and their mammon-led pronouncements, because their cold words bear little or no compassion as they hide in the deadly shadow of the new world regime (I hope these words seem out of date by the time that they are read).

For much of my own life, I felt like an outsider. I found it difficult to gain the inside track in any kind of social circle. I still recall being excluded from our three-man gang in 1958. I was thirteen and a year younger than my two cohort honchos. When they blackballed me, I was absolutely gutted. Across the years, I have felt outside many circles, but a few drinks would ease the loneliness and a few more would yield up the comfort of having a friend to whom I could always turn – my beloved bottle.

Fate dealt me a new hand in 1989 when I met new friends who understood the outside and knew, too, of the inside job and how to find it. My circumstances did not alter, but my view of them began to change. Instead of trying to get out of it, I began to look in. I learned to recognise that acceptance of my, sometimes, aloneness could prevent feelings of loneliness. I have so much around me – my beautiful family, my friends and my work and yet I could get empty feelings of loneliness that used to cripple me and leave me feeling like an outsider.

Writing these few disjointed words this morning helps me feel more inside then out.

I have come to believe in a power greater than myself. I've learned how enabling it is to reach out for help and to offer help. I've learned that to get out of it, all I need to do is reach out.

I can hear the cynics snigger but I understand that too, for there was no more cynical fool than myself, when I stood on the outside.

Christy Moore

THE OUTSIDER

MICHAEL MORIARTY

Perhaps, in a world riven by war, famine and disease, it seems incongruous to have chosen two Zimbabwean cricketers as joint-outsider selections. Yet, what Andrew Flower and Henry Olonga did in February of this year – to denounce from within the brutal and oppressive political regime in their country, as it commenced staging cricket's World Cup – was as courageous as it was almost unheard of in the annals of professional sport.

With very few exceptions, such as Mohammad Ali's refusal to serve in Vietnam and public protests on racial grounds from Cathy Freeman of Australia, and US sprinters Tommie Smith and John Carlos, sports stars have habitually tended to conform to the dictates of the ruling authorities, whether sporting or political. Dictators, whether Hitler, Stalin, or the Argentinean colonels, know the value of sport as propaganda and safety valve, so such conformity has proved especially welcome. Reluctance to rock the boat is usually justified on two grounds, either that star performers focus expertise upon their chosen sport rather than public affairs (as most recently raised by Tiger Woods when asked his view on the Middle East war) or, for rank and file, that it is better to seek to build bridges through sport than use it to fan the flames of larger controversies. Allowance has to be made for each of these, but a stage may, nonetheless, arise where athletes are confronted by ethical or human-rights issues of such magnitude as to make taking total refuge in the cocoon of sport incompatible with self-respect.

It is apparent that Flower and Olonga felt such a stage had been reached, as the initial World Cup fixtures were set to launch in Zimbabwe and South Africa. What had once seemed the possible emergence of a harmonious multi-racial government under a new leader of the newly independent Zimbabwe (from the white-dominated former entity of Rhodesia) had faltered and festered into a tarnished and brutal parody of democracy under the over-protracted regime of that self-same leader, Mr Robert Mugabe. Old scores came to be settled with increasing ferocity by agents of the state, few, if any, of the civil rights taken for granted in Western democracies were honoured in any remotely real form, and any opposition to continuing excesses was ruthlessly dealt with in an ever more divided and demoralised community. But, in sport at least, and particularly in cricket as the game in which Zimbabwe had been accepted as one of the top-flight of competing test-match countries, there was some veneer of harmony, with a mainly white national squad augmented by players from other racial communities. A few notable playing victories had been secured, and it was pleasant for Mr Mugabe as patron of the Zimbabwean Cricket Association, to hope for some more congenial publicity as cricket's premier international competition came to the Harare Stadium close to his presidential palace. Even when England, after much agonising, forfeited their match against Zimbabwe rather than play the match in that country, there seemed little chance of internal dissent amongst the Zimbabwean players.

Flower and Olonga were unlikely comrades in insurrection. Andrew Flower was thirty-four, white and the country's undoubted leading player, once being rated number one in the world, and remaining among a tiny handful of batsmen with an international batting average in excess of fifty. In contrast, Henry Olonga was twenty-six, the first black cricketer to represent his country. He is a gifted singer in classical and popular styles and a person who had nearly chosen acting as his career but, after uncertain early cricketing performances following his initial selection, which probably owed something to planned quota representation, he had settled and improved to become a genuine international fast bowler.

On the morning of 10th February 2003, as the Zimbabwean team took the field for their opening World Cup match against Namibia, it was noticed that Flower and Olonga were wearing black armbands. Immediately before the start, they had issued a joint statement. Having commenced by declaring that they were proud and privileged to be representing their country in the World Cup, they went on to state: 'We are, however, deeply distressed about what is taking place in Zimbabwe… and do not feel that we can take the field without indicating our feelings in a dignified manner.' They continued:

> We cannot in good conscience take to the field and ignore the fact that millions of our compatriots are starving, unemployed and oppressed. We are aware that hundreds of thousands of Zimbabweans may even die in the coming months through a combination of starvation, poverty and Aids. We are aware that many people have been unjustly imprisoned and tortured simply for expressing their opinions about what is happening in the country. We have heard a torrent of racist hate speech directed at minority groups. We are aware that thousands of Zimbabweans are routinely denied their right to freedom of expression. We are aware that people have been murdered, raped, beaten and had their homes destroyed because of their beliefs and that many of those responsible have not been prosecuted. We are also aware that

many patriotic Zimbabweans oppose us even play-ing in the World Cup because of what is happen-ing.

It is impossible to ignore what is happening in Zimbabwe. Although we are just professional cricketers, we do have a conscience and feelings. We believe that if we remain silent that will be taken as a sign that either we do not care or we condone what is happening in Zimbabwe. We believe that it is important to stand up for what is right.

The statement concluded with an indication that each of them considered it an appropriate response to wear a black armband for the duration of the World Cup. 'In doing so, we are mourning the death of democracy in our beloved Zimbabwe. In doing so, we are making a silent plea to those responsible to stop the abuse of human rights in Zimbabwe. In doing so, we pray that our small action may help to restore sanity and dignity to our nation.'

What was at stake for both men was a far cry from the risk taken by an Irish demonstrator who throws a custard pie at a passing cabinet minister: apart from the widespread and well-verified abuses alluded to in their statement, and half of the country's 14 million pop-ulation facing serious food shortages, the main oppo-sition leader was at risk of a possible death sentence if convicted of trying to kill Mugabe. Flower and Olonga were not only effectively forfeiting their professional careers playing for their country, but they were placing their own freedom and safety, along with that of their families, at the gravest personal risk. Their statement was accorded prominent coverage worldwide, and it rele-gated the early World Cup matches to secondary status.

With throngs of international reporters in attendance in Zimbabwe, no immediate reprisals were taken against either player, apart from Olonga's club suspending him for 'disgraceful' conduct in 'taking politics onto the playing field and bringing the game into disrepute', thereby betraying his role as 'a hero and role model to black cricketing communities'. Mr Mugabe was said by an advisor to be 'like a bull incandescent with rage'. The international cricket authorities huffed and puffed with embarrassment, but at least declined to find either man guilty of bringing the game into disrepute.

In the weeks after the controversy, both players reluctantly yielded to the entreaties of their friends and family, and have left Zimbabwe: Flower to fulfil his remaining years as a top professional cricketer in Australia and England and Olonga to pursue recording and other options in London.

As someone who has followed cricket over the years with both enthusiasm and exasperation (although never more than a one-time undistinguished bit player in the unexacting waters of Leinster league cricket) I would have to admit that the game's roll call of heroic outsiders down the years has been a trifle sparse. However, in acting as they did, Andy Flower and Henry Olonga have surely struck more than a small blow in redressing that balance.

Michael Moriarty

TWO LEFT FEET

VINCENT MURPHY

'What team do you support?' I was asked.

'None,' I replied.

'You can't support none. You have to have a team,' I was told.

I was in primary school in Fethard in Tipperary in the 1970s. Everybody had a favourite soccer team. Most of the lads in the class supported either Manchester United or Liverpool. A few went for Arsenal and Leeds. I had no interest in soccer. It made me feel different. I much preferred to hide away somewhere and read a book or a comic. I was a skinny little fellow with two left feet and absolutely no aptitude for sports. When teams were being picked at break time, I was usually the last to be picked. If the numbers weren't even, I often didn't get picked at all. This suited me fine. It meant that I could slip away and hide in a book. This I did in private as I didn't want to be called a sissy.

One day, sick of telling people that I didn't support any team, I decided to pick one. I still knew nothing about the game and cared even less, but I did want to fit in. So I picked Fourth Division Aldershot. My uncle lives there so, to me, that was as good a reason as any to pick them. I knew absolutely nothing about them, except that they went bankrupt, which a soccer fan informed me one day. I replaced them with Scunthorpe because I liked the name. I didn't make a very good job of fitting in. I should have picked a team from the First Division that everybody knew about.

The whole soccer episode was an early example of society expecting an individual to conform. It makes life easier if you do. We live in a world where people want to put you into a category or place you in a group.

Wear a Man United jersey and you belong to a group. If we look around us, we can see people with similar occupations or hobbies slotting into groups. Golfers tend to dress the same, as do businessmen, soldiers, hippies, ravers, punks, priests and nuns. The outsider often wears one of these uniforms to try and fit in.

My soccer incident didn't scar me for life, but it did highlight a sense of difference between people. Some people aren't able to fit in. I regularly see those people when I'm working in the pub. They are often on their own. People react to them in different ways. Some make an effort to speak to them, some tolerate them and some ignore them. Occasionally, some turn on them, normally when a group of like-minded individuals reject the person. It's just the schoolyard transferred to the pub.

These people come from all walks of life. They're not always the stereotypical outsider. I've heard people refer to a highly intelligent person as 'an educated fool' because he or she doesn't have anything in common with the people around them. This person may not be able to discuss the latest development in *Fair City* or may not be *au fait* with the team positions in the Premiership, so he or she is marked as an outsider.

There are, of course, the more obvious people. There are the 'Knights of the Road'. These people, mainly men, wander around Ireland from hostel to hostel, staying in charity lodgings for as long as the managers of the hostels allow them to stay. In some places it's one night, in others it's two or three. Often they don't get to a hostel, so a hay barn often becomes their bed for the night. Many have developed problems with drink. One man used to come into the bar and beg for money for food. As soon as he had enough collected, he would order a pint and sip it in the seat behind the fire in the pub for a few hours. He minded his own business, but had a hawk's eye for customers who left without finishing their drinks. These slops were added to his glass. He would talk away to himself until closing time and then head for a hay barn for the night. The following day, he would get a dinner from the nuns in the local convent before setting off for his next stop.

Other less obvious people just find it difficult to start up or enter a conversation. We all know people who can walk into a room and can chat to everybody within a few minutes, but there are those who just can't. They often need help. Sometimes it takes the smallest gesture. A smile, a nod or a simple hello can be the spark to ignite a person.

One customer used to call regularly. He was well dressed, well spoken and never short of money. He had a ritual of ordering his whiskey and a beer, sitting on a particular seat, smoking his cigarettes and reading his paper. He never spoke, except to reorder his drink. One day, there was only the two of us in the bar. I can't remember what started the conversation, but it was like opening a floodgate. The man was well travelled, having worked all over the world, from Siberia to Africa, and he had some great stories to tell. Often, because of the harsh environments in which he worked, he closed himself off from the others around him to become less conspicuous. His work made him an outsider.

The other side of my working life is a little unusual to some people. I run the family undertaking business. This gives me an insight into a part of Irish life that the majority of people will never experience. I get to see beyond the façade that people throw up to protect themselves.

As I write, in the twenty-first century, there are people living in nineteenth-century conditions in this country. These people aren't always poor people – in fact some have assets worth large amounts of money. Many of these people grew up in a country that was very different to the Ireland of today. They lived in an environment where it was necessary to be frugal. Ireland prior to the 1970s was very much a nation of small farm holdings. Money wasn't easy to accumulate and, when it was gathered, it was saved for the rainy day, which could come at any time. People lived in fear of the poorhouse. There was a stigma attached to ending one's life in the poorhouse, so some people hoarded every penny. Many died with cash saved for the rainy day hidden in biscuit tins, under mattresses, in books or in holes in the wall. For some, this was the only way. Work was often more important than education, so many left school with few or no literacy skills. They couldn't sign their name on a cheque and didn't want anyone else to know it. Often they were too proud to rent or sell land. They wouldn't hand it over to the next generation, as many had placed their elderly relatives in the poorhouse as soon as the land was handed over.

Not so long ago I collected a man from a hovel. There were holes in the walls. Everything was filthy. The man himself obviously hadn't had a wash in many years. I brought him to the mortuary to be embalmed as his next of kin all lived overseas. The embalmer was busy, so he asked me to return later that evening. When I returned a few hours later, I saw a different man on the mortuary slab.

The embalmer had washed the deceased seven times to get the dirt off of him.

'Look at his hair,' he said.

The black-haired man, that I had brought to be embalmed, had a fine head of silvery grey hair. When the neighbours saw him in the coffin the following day, they said that he looked like his younger self. The man had gradually retreated from mainstream society, where he died in squalor. There are many more like him. They might live closer to you than you think. Some won't let you help them. Some may not be able to communicate their cry for help. You could try a nod or a smile or a hello. It might make all the difference.

Vincent Murphy

DR NOËL BROWNE

DAVID NELIGAN

In the general election in 1949, which ended the first sixteen years of Fianna Fáil rule, a virtually unknown outsider was elected in Dublin South East for a new political party – Clann na Poblachta – and became Minister for Health on his first day in the Dáil at the age of thirty-two. He was Dr Noël Browne, regarded by people across the political spectrum as the finest Minister for Health ever, serving from 1948–1951.

He was elected because of his fight against tuberculosis, which had reached almost epidemic proportions – 4,000 people a year were dying of it – and there was terror in the land because of its appalling infectiousness.

The 1946 Census of Population had also starkly exposed the grossly unequal society that the politicians had presided over since the foundation of the State – the infant mortality rate in Dublin, for example, was 133 per 1,000 in the lower income group compared with 29 per 1,000 in the higher income group.

By the time, in 1951, that an unholy alliance of the perennially greedy medical profession, the Catholic Church – at its most powerful and most obscurantist – and the equally perennially craven and cowardly political establishment had destroyed his political career, the TB epidemic had been defeated. Probably the greatest single political achievement of any minister in the history of the State. He became a hero, especially to the poor in Dublin who saw, in the period from 1948 to 1953, an 83 per cent decline in TB deaths amongst children in the city.

Dr Browne achieved his success by using his extraordinary political skills forged by a remarkable childhood and adolescence including a near-fatal infection with tuberculosis.

The story of Browne's extraordinary and moving early life is almost beyond fiction, as he described in an interview for the *Journal of Irish Literature* in May 1978:

> My parents both died of TB early on. My father died first, a young man... my mother was left with £100 and seven of us. A lovely gentle person – she was quite frequently in terrible pain, crying and all that... we weren't able to help her. We couldn't afford a doctor... our wonderful sister, Eileen, left school at 14 and went to England and then brought us all over... mother died shortly after we arrived, kind of relieved, poor lady, she couldn't take it any more. That left its mark on one.

Did it what!

As he said in an interview late in life, 'I have been unable, when I see what I feel is human suffering or degradation, humiliation or pain, or avoidable unhappiness, to pass by on the other side.'

The subsequent death of Eileen, also from TB, and of his hunchbacked brother, Jody, whose pauper's grave was never found, his extraordinary luck in meeting people who sent him as a young orphaned Irish boy to a top English Jesuit school, and his meeting there a son of the generous Chance family, part owners of Independent Newspapers, who later put him through Trinity medical school, is the stuff of fairy tales. Luck, perhaps, but Browne's extraordinary charisma was obviously present even as a boy.

Never has a politician been elected in this country who fulfilled so many of the expectations of those who put him there. He was a consummate politician.

He built hospitals and sanatoriums all over Ireland, produced a better BCG vaccination scheme than the British, started the blood transfusion service, increased mass radiography and laboratory testing and many other improvements. '*Si monumentum requiris circumspice*' ('If you wish to remember him, look about you').

What was unique in Ireland then – and indeed now – was the speed with which it all happened. He visited the county homes – he called them workhouses – 'one bath with cold tap for 200 people', 'food poured into vats like in Dickens' time' and, as he recounted in his scintillating autobiography *Against the Tide*, a workhouse in Mullingar where the children were distinguished by wearing jerkins with their numbers on the back. He came back to the Dáil appalled and called on de Valera to resign.

The State, in 1948, had minimal resources after the Second World War and decades of inept political mismanagement with the poverty-stricken population facing emigration or starvation. Noël Browne's, and Clann's, progressive social policies created a more dynamic atmosphere than the feeble Irish Labour Party had ever been able to create since the days of James Connolly.

As he said in *Against the Tide*:

With few exceptions, it is as difficult for a member of the working class in the Republic to leave that class, with all its limitations and penalties, as for a camel to pass through the eye of a needle. The question needs to be posed as to how in a society where the working classes constitute the vast majority of an electorate they continue to elect politicians who maintain an educational system which so blatantly discriminates against them and their children? Such discrimination persists in the health services, in employment, in housing, in rec-

reation, against women and in living conditions
among the aged. Because of this obvious anomaly,
the thoughtful have long since shed the fiction
that through our system of parliamentary democracy we have an effective instrument of popular
will. As in the Aesop fable of the Fox and the
Crow, the middle class continues to hold power
and to use it so that it is retained.

His monumental achievement in eradicating TB was,
however, to be overshadowed by the controversy over
his new health bill. In 1947, Dr James Ryan, the then
Fianna Fáil Minister of Health, had passed the Health
Bill 1947, allowing a comprehensive mother and child
health service free of all charges to the patient. No Dáil
deputy dissented, though James Dillon, later leader of
Fine Gael, stopped it in the courts.

With the change of government, Noël Browne, as
the new minister, decided to implement this necessary
improvement in health care that was to be offered as a
Mother and Child Scheme without a means test – a national health service for women and children up to the
age of sixteen in a country that had the highest infant
and maternal mortality in Europe. This led to his down-
fall and the dissolution of the first coalition government, but it changed the political face of Ireland for
ever.

The Catholic Church, in the person of Archbishop
McQuaid, decided, incredibly, that free medical care was
against Catholic teaching. The Church's alliance with the
medical profession – whose members were, as always,
more interested in their wallets than the condition of
the poor – and the compliant and supine Fine Gael-led
government – including the shameful collaboration of
the Labour Party – defeated what is still a much-needed
medical scheme fifty years on.

The context within which this fundamental battle was fought was one in which the Catholic Church effectively controlled the government, allowing no social advances in areas such as adoption – there were 4,000 children in foster homes supervised by untrained officials, the effects of which are only now coming to light.

We had become a theocratic state ruled over by a prelate, John Charles McQuaid, amongst whose many edicts were a prohibition on nuns helping families where the mother was hospitalised with TB as it would 'give scandal'; the banning of mixed schools, and the apartheid in education, which persists to this day. When he was president of Blackrock College, McQuaid had disapproved of the National Athletics Association's decision to allow women to compete in track and field events because they would wear shorts – writing to them that 'no boy from my college will take part in any athletics controlled by your organisation at which women will compete, no matter what attire they adopt'; the new tampon, Tampax, was banned for a time as he said they could 'stimulate girls of an impressionable age'; the prohibition under pain of mortal sin – reaffirmed every year from the altars – on Catholics attending Trinity College and the naked attempt to promote UCD as the Catholic university where many of the staff and professors were either clerics or sycophants appointed with his approval and to do his bidding. Censorship of books and films was so all-encompassing that virtually all our best writers emigrated making us the laughing-stock of the world.

Noël Browne, at that time, stood virtually alone in the Dáil against this incredible tyranny. Outsider indeed.

With the defeat of Dr Browne's Mother and Child Scheme and his forced resignation, the Catholic Church, winning the battle but losing the war, suffered a watershed from which it has never recovered. The main fact,

which often goes in danger of being lost in the mael-
strom, was that an unelected body, the Catholic hierarchy, although entitled to its view, had tried to dictate the
social policy of a sovereign state. Seán ÓFaoláin put it
succinctly in *The Bell:* 'The Browne case shows we have
two parliaments – a parliament at Maynooth and a parliament in Dublin. The Dáil proposes; Maynooth dis-
poses. When up against the Second Parliament, the Dáil
has only one right of decision: the right to surrender.'

As Dr Browne said in an interview with Kurt Jacob-
sen in 1978, 'the absurdity was that north of the border
in Belfast the archbishop himself could get sick under a
State-socialised scheme while ten miles south of the border it was a sin.'

I believe if Browne had not exposed the appalling
collusion between the Taoiseach, John A Costello, and
Archbishop McQuaid, we would have had many more
years of secret government and the continuation of the
hated dispensary system based on poor law medicine.
As it was, for many years Dr Browne, amongst others,
led the fight for the legal right to contraception and divorce against a craven political establishment, leading
as always from behind, terrified of another 'belt of a
crozier'.

Times don't change much; housing, the homeless,
the health services, conditions in our prisons and mental hospitals are all major problems still with us. Yet we
have passed through the richest phase in our history,
reaching and exceeding the European average for income levels. Our journalists and politicians are not the
subservient poltroons they once were – they are both
honourable professions – yet why so little change?

Noël's subsequent political adventures are a political
history of the times. After the fall of the first coalition,
he was re-elected as an independent with his highest
vote ever. The poor of Dublin knew who was looking

out for them even if the politicians and the Church didn't.

Later, when he formed the National Progressive Democrats with the other finest politician I ever met, Jack McQuillan, they were described by Seán Lemass as the 'only real opposition'. Later still, he joined the Labour Party in its short-lived socially crusading phase in the 1960s.

In 1971, in response to an attack from Browne, the Labour Party issued a statement saying they would never support the supply of contraceptives in slot machines or any other way to unmarried people – on a par surely with Charles Haughey's subsequent bill to supply them solely to married couples – and only with a doctor's prescription – his infamous 'Irish solution to an Irish problem'. Of such imbecilities is Irish political life made.

Browne became an independent senator for Trinity in 1973 having declined to stand for the proposed coalition programme, which became a uniquely unpopular government. He stayed on as a TD for the Socialist Labour Party until 1982 and never ceased to keep an interest in politics. I talked to him ten days before he died at the age of eighty-three in 1997 and he fulminated at what had become the 'corporate state'.

It has been fashionable to call him a failed politician and I even saw a recent headline calling him, hilariously, a 'tortured soul'. No tortured soul he – quite the opposite, being wonderfully witty company – and his political career, though at great personal cost to him, was a success in real terms. He didn't care about his personal battering and he left life with almost as few possessions as he came into it, watched over and still watched over, by his beloved Phyllis, content and at peace.

Outsider, hero, we should not forget him.

David Neligan

MY BROTHER MARTIN

My brother Martin is a priest in South Africa. Prior to this, he worked in Kenya. Since he arrived in South Africa in 1992, much has changed. Or has it?

In 2000, I visited him and saw for myself what 'missionaries' do. Although he lives in a comfortable house, only 15 kilometres away the contrast is stark. Heavy rain and subsequent floods have washed away roads and houses.

We visited some of the villages and the sights were pitiful. People standing in what remained of their mud huts bereft of any possessions, yet managing a handshake and a smile. Some expressed surprise that a 'European' had come to visit. They understood when I was introduced as Martin's 'blood brother'. Somehow Martin was accepted as one of their own. Later, I understood why.

Martin has a capacity to genuinely assume that people are basically 'good'. This doesn't blind him to people's greed and self-centredness – the consequences of which he is only too aware. But he has an ease and openness that is so affecting. People feel accepted by him no matter what. There is no air of dogma or righteousness about him, but there is 'I was thirsty and you gave me drink'. Because he doesn't look for complications, he knows freedom and self-expression in their truest sense.

What sustains his commitment is this optimistic belief in the basic goodness of humanity. He has touched people in real ways, including Flora who has a chronic bone infection in her leg. For the past three years, she has been unable to walk. She lives in a tin shed with her daughter and handicapped son. They swelter in the heat of the day and freeze in the cold of night. Her husband

has long since left her and she has no means of support. Martin visits her weekly, providing food.

Anna never learned to read or write and a succession
of failed relationships have left her lonely. The fact that
she is dying of Aids has turned her into an outsider.
Martin, however, spotted her will and spirit to survive.
She is now a Minister of the Eucharist.

While with my brother, I saw many other instances
of 'a candle being lit rather than cursing the darkness'.

Martin is himself, he is Irish. He understands people's struggles. His tastes are his own. This was affirmed
to me one evening when we were sitting outside his
house listening to Bridie Gallagher singing 'The Homes
of Donegal' and 'Cutting the Corn at Creeslagh'. We
looked at each other, there were tears in our eyes and I
said to my brother – the voluntary outsider –'*Is faid ó
bhaile atá muid.*'

John J O'Connor

THE PUZZLE OF
INDIVIDUAL DIFFERENCE

PADRAIG O'MORAIN

There was a certain point in my childhood when I began to realise that there is a difference between what people say *to* other people and what they say *about* them. While I cannot remember the incident that brought this realisation to me, I certainly remember the sense of puzzlement I felt at the time. It was bad enough that people seemed to think one thing, for instance that so-and-so was a great fellow altogether, and that they then turned out to think another, i.e. that so-and-so was a pest and a nuisance and a blight on humanity.

But what really struck me was the enormous show of sincerity with which they expressed both points of view. Given that show of sincerity, how could you really figure out what was going on in people's heads? What was true and what was not true?

That moment of puzzlement has never ended. I still don't know what is going on in other people's heads and I'm not always too sure what's going on in my own. Moreover, I don't really want to find out. I am one of those people who prefers the journey to the destination and I am entirely happy to live in a state of puzzlement.

On that journey, I came across the work of Dr William Glasser and that is what I want to write about here. Glasser is an American psychiatrist, born in 1925, who developed an approach called Choice Theory, which is based firmly in the sort of respect for diversity that Trust so greatly exemplifies.

Glasser is an absolute believer in individuality, in our right to make choices and in the idea that all behaviour, however odd it may appear, makes sense. I'll explain more of that later, but the first thing to be said about

Glasser is that he has never been afraid to be an outsider.

Back in the late 1950s and early 1960s, he decided he
did not believe in the existence of mental illness – a
pretty startling (though not unheard of) opinion for a
psychiatrist working in a mental hospital to hold. Today
he holds the same view – and has not the slightest hesi-
tation in defending it whether in the United States or on
his visits to Ireland. He also – and this almost gets him
more disapproval than his opinions on mental illness –
has rejected the approach to psychology developed by
Freud and others that depends enormously on going
back into the past. Glasser has no interest in going back
into the past with the people he is treating, except briefly
for the purpose of finding their successes and their
strengths to build on. He also manages to annoy large
numbers of people by insisting that we make choices all
the time, that our motivations come from inside us and
not from outside.

In a society characterised by a sort of worship of
victimhood, in which many of us like to think that other
people have ruined our lives and ought to pay for it,
Glasser's approach does not go down at all well. So why
am I inspired by this man's theories? Why is it that many
teachers, especially career guidance teachers, in this country have studied his theories and his counselling method,
called Reality Therapy? Why is his approach so popular
among drug-treatment workers? It is because, even if
you don't agree with everything he says – and I don't –
Glasser's approach, if implemented, would result in
immeasurably greater respect for the individual than
there is now.

Glasser says that all behaviour makes sense, that everybody is trying to meet their needs all the time. These
needs he sums up as belonging, freedom, power, fun
and survival. Here's the crucial thing though: everybody

has their own particular way of meeting those needs and that way, however quirky, should be respected so long as it doesn't infringe on other people's ability to meet their legitimate needs. He also believes that the fundamental problem when things go wrong for us is that our relationships are unsatisfactory.

How does all this work in the real world? Suppose a person lives on the streets, with all its attendant problems. How would that make sense or meet a person's needs? I would imagine that the person's need for belonging is met by being with other people who live on the streets and by going to meal centres and to places like Trust. What about the need for freedom? Perhaps the person on the streets has gained freedom from mental or physical abuse or, in some cases, unfortunately, from their responsibilities towards their families.

Then there is the need for power. This can be thought of as a need for winning, getting your way, achievement, being worthwhile, being respected. Perhaps the very act of survival brings a sense of achievement with it for people on the streets. Perhaps, also, there are those who meet their power need by bossing others about. You could also get a feeling of power through drinking. Glasser believes that the big attraction of alcohol is that it give us a false feeling of control. Well, sometimes a false feeling of control is better than no feeling of control at all – though it must be remembered that, ultimately, this false feeling of control can be destructive.

What about fun, enjoyment? Where would you get that on the streets? I don't know because I've never lived that life. But people have a laugh when they're together and, if you go into a place like Trust, I can promise you that you will hear a lot of laughter. And survival? Well, maybe some of those on the streets survived by getting out of their homes. But they have to survive on the streets too: perhaps share a doorway with someone else, keep your money beneath you, sleep in a place where no one will find you. You can see how people are meeting their needs, even in the dangerous environment of the streets.

For many, perhaps most, though, there is a great deal of pain in this way of meeting their needs. So why choose this way? This is where relationships come in. For many, in my experience of interviewing people as a journalist, there has been a terrible rupture of relationships and it is this that has led them here.

I think of the man taken away from his family because, as a child, he went into a church to smoke a cigarette surreptitiously, set the church on fire, and was sent to an institution where he suffered vicious sexual abuse and saw other children being abused too. That abuse tore the whole notion of relationships to shreds for that man and now he cannot be with people. Or I think of a girl who prefers a doorway to a foul-mouthed, bullying stepfather; of a boy whose way of treating his parents and siblings is so bad they have thrown him out. Glasser would say that all these people are doing their best to meet their needs at any given time. But some of these ways, he would argue, are ineffective and people will do better if they make better choices.

The key thing here is to be able to respect other people's legitimate choices. For instance, I might think you would be better off in a corporation flat than in a hostel. I might be wrong. You might choose to leave the flat, because you're there staring at the four walls with nothing to do, and you might be better off in a hostel because you would, at least, have company. This business of individual choice is fundamentally important.

I knew a man who got compensation for some accident or other and who, when asked what he would do with the money replied, 'I'm thinking of getting a pair of boots', and he meant it. Another man I know of, who won the Lotto, takes a taxi every day to a nearby town, drinks all day and takes a taxi home. I know a person who is rich through her own efforts and has divided up her money among members of her family. I know of another man who won a million, keeps a room in a hotel with a well-stocked bar, and spends his time at dances in the same hotel inviting women up for drinks. Individual choice. Glasser would say that the above choices might not be yours but they are perfectly valid for the people making them.

We all have different ways of meeting our needs. One of my grandmothers liked Fry's Chocolate Cream bars and I liked Cadbury's chocolate bars. My uncle likes a bottle of Guinness and a large Haig and I like a glass of red wine. My brothers can sit for hours watching a grand prix and I would rather watch a video of *Men in Black*. My wife wants her steak well done, I want mine medium and someone else wants it bleeding.

Different ways of meeting our needs, different wants. Glasser says that, if you take all the different things you want, from Mars Bars to world peace, you can describe them as your Quality World. I suppose the great lesson I take from Glasser is the importance of accepting the other person's Quality World and of being prepared to expect that they will accept mine. The refusal to accept the other person's Quality World, because it is different, is a great source of human misery.

Indeed, Dr Abraham Low, who founded the Recovery organisation around 1940 (it's still going strong) saw this insistence on being right, this rejection of the other person's way, as a cause of extreme mental distress in those who were the victims of this kind of bullying.

As I write this, I realise that, when you walk into Trust, you walk into a world in which differences are accepted, in which you can be as odd as you like because we're all a bit odd anyhow and in which a high value is placed on respecting other people's choices. In other words, though it is a jargon-free environment, Trust is a place in which your Quality World is respected. Dr William Glasser has never, I am sure, heard of Trust. I am also sure he would feel at home there and that all those who meet in Trust would feel at home with him.

As I said at the start, I *have* never, and *will* never, figure out what goes on in people's heads, including my own. But I am glad that my journey has brought me in contact with Glasser, Trust and other people who stand out in my lifetime as contributing towards making the journey worthwhile.

Padraig O'Morain

THOUGHTS

MARY O'ROURKE

In deciding about a topic for this piece, I decided on writing from a highly personal point of view. It is fully correct that society should seek to have inclusion at the centre of all of its endeavours, whether those endeavours be commercial, educational, social, cultural or in any other area of life.

I have thought long and hard about this. We long for inclusion. Thinking back to primary school days, you always wanted to be 'part of the gang' so to speak and were always envious of the child who was ringleader, to whom others flocked and admired. Sometimes being part of the gang was being part of that inclusive spirit but, in the time-old cruelty of childhood, one often felt left out, discarded, a nobody. But this is all part of growing up, of the maturing process so to speak. Indeed, as I write this, I repeat again what we have all said at various times of our lives: if only I had known of that experience at a different age. But, of course, we never do. In fact, we have to learn through experience.

Learning through experience and maturity shows us that we cannot ever be completely inclusive. I think a small part of us must always remain private and solitary. When we fall in love, we long to share with our beloved every thought, every word, every action, every minute of every hour of every day of every week of every month of every year. We ache for this fellow feeling and the sharing of every emotion. This, of course, would be the perfect state here on earth, but it isn't possible. I would suggest that a sense of identity and purpose and love is best served by keeping a portion of oneself to oneself.

There are recurrent moments in your life when it is right that you are alone for reflection, for pondering on issues and for thinking forward. Reading gives you great time for this. During my time of rearing young children, and later in my teaching career in secondary school, I always encouraged young people to read. In fact, I constantly repeated to them to read anything. Obviously, I encouraged more strongly the reading of good books and poetry and plays and articles in periodicals and newspapers but, in the end, it always came down to wanting to foster a real love of reading in every young person. Thus fostered, that habit and love of reading will stay with you and you will find that books are friends who never leave you and in whose pages you will find constant delight. Of course, a love of books can be inclusive because you can share your delight, pass on your books, share the views, talk about the characters, envisage more exotic worlds, but the very best of reading is done by yourself and to yourself.

If you don't give ourselves time for reflection alone, how can your mind and your spirit thrive? What I am trying to put forward is how you can be inclusive and yet be happy to be alone in the knowledge that you share an inclusive society and the comfort that that gives you. But there is an equal need for the comfort of one's own company and delight in that company.

In times of great sorrow, friends, relations, acquaintances and workmates are great help to temper your sorrow and to lead you out from what seems an endless abyss. And yet, you need to be alone, you need to think through your sorrow, you need to reflect on your sorrow, to think of the person, to work your way through it and so to keep always those happy memories in a private part of your mind and being where you can gain happiness from that deep inner sanctuary of yourself which you have kept to yourself for yourself.

We all know the poem 'Four Ducks on a Pond':

Four ducks on a pond,
A grass bank beyond,
A blue sky of spring,
White birds on the wing:
What a little thing
To remember for years–
To remember with tears!

Allingham's feelings are expressed in somewhat grander language by William Wordsworth:

When oft upon my couch I lie in vacant or in
    pensive mood
They flash upon that inward eye which is the bliss
    of solitude.
And then my heart with pleasure fills and dances
    with the daffodils.

Both of these poets are describing what Wordsworth called 'emotions recollected in tranquillity', and this tranquil re-living of emotions gives all of us solace and comfort and time on our own to wallow, if you like, in that tranquility.

I was listening recently to John Quinn giving the 'Thought for the Day' on early-morning RTÉ Radio – John Quinn who penned the beautiful *Letters to Olive* following the untimely and so very poignant death of his dear wife, Olive. He was talking on the fact that children no longer have time have to meander in life.

When you look back on childhood, there seemed always to be plenty of time to kick stones on the road, to go off swimming with your friends, to run up and down hills and shout with joy and to walk by the hedges gathering blackberries – plenty of time to chat and talk and in general to meander. (What a lovely word meander is, taken from the name of a river in Asia Minor.)

Now it seems that life is crowding us all out – no time to meander, no time to reflect, no time, no time, no time. No time for the 'still sad music of humanity' to echo and re-echo within us.

So my thought for the day is that there should be inclusivity, yes, but that each of us as individuals should keep a bit of ourselves *for* ourselves.

Mary O'Rourke

OUTSIDER

MICHEAL O'SIADHAIL

A sheltered arch or where underground
kitchens of an inn sent
through grids of pavement grating
the warmth of the ass's breath —
Where did last night's Christ lie down?

Every morning for months I watched
a man I might have been,
about my age and bearded too,
his face blotched crimson
with cheap wine and sleeping rough.

He walked the far side of the street
always hurrying somewhere;
a father who couldn't praise, I wondered,
or what had blurred his star?
For months our eyes never met,

though the street between us was narrow,
until that eve he crossed.
'Some help,' he said, but it must have been
my double's eyes that asked
where would He lie down tomorrow?

An old outsider within me winced,
shook him off and fled;
that street between was so narrow —
I chose the inn and was afraid.
I'm sure I've never seen him since —
but tomorrow when carafes go round

a lone presence will pass
tremors through our frail togetherness;
again those eyes will ask
where did last night's Christ lie down?

Micheal O'Siadhail

JIM CONNOLLY: FROM BANDLEADER TO COMMUNITY ACTIVIST

NORA OWEN

Jim Connolly is the founder of Rural Resettlement Ireland (RRI), which helps people from the cities or large towns to resettle in rural Ireland. Jim's idea of thirty years made him an outsider because many thought he was mad to think he could persuade 'city-slickers' to move to remote places and thereby help to reverse the flight from the land that was leading to the closure of schools and businesses and the death of the dispersed villages of Ireland.

Jim Connolly has succeeded in both these objectives. Over 500 families, including 1,000 children, have been moved by RRI. And every day brings letters and phone calls asking for help to move from the pressures of city life. Most letters come from women and nearly all voice the same reason for moving – 'for the sake of the children'.

Jim says it is heartbreaking to read some of these letters filled with fears that children growing up in the huge suburban estates will get involved in crime or drugs or will drop out of school because their pals are doing so. Many of the people moving are unemployed and RRI is careful to stress that they cannot guarantee a job. However, one of the unforeseen advantages of the scheme is that many parents have availed of FÁS and other training courses and are now employed or running their own businesses, something they all admit they wouldn't be doing if they had stayed in the city. Children are staying in school. In fact, the arrival of new families with children in Doonaha, County Clare, has resulted in saving the school threatened with closure –

and it is now expanding to a two-teacher school. Already some of the early movers are completing third-level courses. Even some weddings are planned between sons and daughters of rural farmers and their 'new' neighbours, thereby ensuring another rural household.

Jim Connolly could play you a tune on his trumpet, he could teach you to be an artist or he could sculpt you a 20-foot statue, such is his talent, and he has earned his living from all these talents. But his lifelong interest has been in community work. He was working as bandleader of The Monarchs Showband with Tommy Drennan in the 1950s and early 1960s. He met and married his Donegal-born wife, Kathleen, after a whirlwind romance and moved to Donegal and, as he says himself, he 'retired' into teaching art away from the hectic life of showbands. He saw at first hand the exodus from the rural parts of Donegal to the towns and cities and was particularly alarmed by a Foras Forbaithe Report in the early 1960s that forecast that south Donegal would be completely depopulated in forty years if efforts were not made to bring employment and services to the region. He got involved and was inspired by the work of the great Fr McDyer of Glencolmcille.

It was then that Jim first had the idea that it should be possible to use the increasing number of empty houses for relieving the ever-increasing housing lists in Dublin and other cities. However, like the singer Val Doonican, of whom it is said 'he was an overnight success after twenty years!', Jim's plan only became a reality in 1990 after thirty years, by which time Jim and his family were living in Kilbaha, County Clare.

He did an interview on the *Gay Byrne Radio Show*, spelling out his proposals to find houses for people to settle in remote areas of Clare and elsewhere and, within two hours, he had received 100 phone calls and the letters began to pour in in their dozens. In that first year, Jim helped seven families to move, driving them around himself and identifying houses they could rent. For the next twelve years, Jim and a group of dedicated people worked voluntarily helping to resettle over 500 families from the small beginning in 1990. RRI now has five full-time employees.

It has not all been plain sailing for Jim and his volunteer group. Because of the novel approach to rehousing people, none of the rules and regulations of county councils and the Department of Environment seem to fit RRI's plans. Jim spent many frustrating hours explaining and cajoling the powers that be that new rules were required to suit his scheme. Most of the families moving were giving back their council houses to the council, but no allowance was made by the councils to their former tenants. It is only in the last two years that RRI now receives ₤3,000 for each house surrendered and with these monies and a small annual grant from the Department of Environment, RRI can offer backup services to their families when they move. Dublin Corporation now provides a small office in the Civic Offices in Fishamble Street where an RRI employee can provide information each day.

Not satisfied with what he has already achieved, Jim and his team have just received planning permission for seven new houses in County Clare. These form part of the RRI Rental Subsidy Social Housing Scheme, which was announced by Minister Robert Molloy in 2001.

Currently, most families who have resettled are renting houses and security of tenure is still a worry. To overcome this problem, the Social Housing Scheme will enable people to be tenants but they will get tenure for life from RRI. This latest venture is to operate over five counties but as people have already been resettled in counties Clare, Leitrim, Mayo, Donegal, Limerick and Kerry, there is no doubt that Jim won't stop at five! Even this latest idea has run into problems due to the planning policies of some counties whereby only locals can build in rural areas, but Jim is once again battling the authorities to overcome this setback, and on his past record he is bound to succeed.

Jim Connolly is a mould-breaker in the best sense of the expression. He has been determined and dogged in fighting bureaucracy and some opposition in order to see his ideas become a reality. He believes that where one lives can define and shape what the future holds by way of opportunities. Housing policies can ghettoise or liberate families and, as an example of this, he points out how the 'wrong address' can prevent a person from getting employment. He passionately believes that without better social mix in housing, such discrimination will continue. He has seen, at first hand, the difference it has made to people's confidence and happiness to be accepted for themselves and for the part they play in a community rather than to be shunned because of their address.

For me, Jim Connolly epitomises a true modern-day patriot with his passion to ensure that rural Ireland does not die but is enriched instead by people who are encouraged to return to the countryside and make new lives for themselves. He shows no sign of retiring, though he has reached an age where most others are doing so, and he will continue to challenge the politicians, the departments and county councils to adapt the rules and regulations and housing policies so that they best suit the needs of those requiring housing or an opportunity to make a new start.

Nora Owen

COMING IN

Our Lady of Victories. 'Yeah! Sure,' he thought, victory over him.

Despite the fact that he had never been inside a Catholic church in his life, Julian ran as fast as he could through the doors when he was chased by the boys from the 'Noggin.

He had got off the bus from school and was heading for the gate to his house when they spotted him and came charging. 'Proddy dog! Proddy dog!'

He took off in the direction of the only refuge he could see, the church. As he burst in the doors, the priest was standing in the aisle. 'Out with ye, ye blackguards, out to hell with all of ye,' he shouted as he came down the aisle towards them.

Julian stood trapped between the priest in his swirling black robes who was fast approaching him and the gang of four who blocked the doorway behind him.

Luckily the priest recognised some of them and shouted at them. 'Murphy! Kelly! Get out of here and stop your play-acting.'

Fortunately for Julian, the fear they had of the priest outweighed any pleasure they may have had in keeping him cornered. They ran out.

Trying to time his exit, Julian hung on as long as he dared under the approaching glare of the priest and, at the last minute, turned and ran out the door into the bright sunlight.

Dazzled by the brightness, he did not spot them as he came out the door, and the first he knew of their presence was when a fist exploded on his ear.

It was shocking.

He had never been hit in anger like this before. Sure

he had felt the lash of a wooden spoon on his behind from time to time, but never had a fellow human being deliberately made a fist of his hand and punched him in the face.

He did the worst thing he could have done, he burst into tears.

They roared in triumph,

'Cry baby, cry baby.'

'Proddy dog's a cry baby.'

'That will teach you for going into our church,' and then, as they circled him, one of them threw in the final jibe, 'and Martin Luther was the most evil person who ever lived.'

He ran home, they didn't even bother following him. They knew he was mortally wounded and was not worth chasing.

He never knew he was different till then.

He was seven, and he had no idea who Martin Luther was.

His family had recently moved to Glenageary. The address was Glenageary, but it was so close to Sally-noggin it made no difference.

Well, it should have made no difference, but it did.

Being Protestant and living in a big house were two red rags to the local lads. Not that his family owned the big house, they simply lived in one corner of it.

Glenageary House had been *The Big House* in its day but, like its owners, it had fallen on hard times and was now in decline. It was set out in flats. Its grounds were being gradually sold off, plot by plot, and the new houses that sprung up were surrounding their prey slowly, closing in for the kill.

That afternoon as Julian lay sobbing on his bed, he felt the house crying with him.

From then on, he was always watching over his shoulder.

Never walking home after dark.

Phoning for a lift if caught at a friend's house too late.

This was Ireland in the 1960s.

No peace and love as Catholics re-established themselves after generations of being the underdogs in their own land.

He got on with things and, of course, life wasn't always miserable. There were the long summers spent swimming in Dún Laoghaire baths, conker fights and Christmases.

But then came the time came for secondary school.

Determined not to have Julian go through any more problems, his parents decided that he should go to a school in town, in Dublin, where he would be removed from the daily taunts of his suburban tormentors.

Take the outsider away and put him amongst his own.

Being enrolled in a Protestant school should have been the solution. Being enrolled in a Protestant Grammar and Choir School should have been the perfect solution.

But his own turned out to disown him.

He discovered, to his horror, that, having made the move, he was still an outsider.

He found himself shunned and rejected amongst inner-city, working-class Protestants who resented this posh kid from Glenageary (suddenly Glenageary was miles from Sallynoggin).

In some ways what happened there was worse. Its always harder when your own turn on you, at least in the 'Noggin you understood why they hated you, it was almost expected of them.

He grew to dread school breaks. The jeering, the kicks, the grinding down of his spirit. He lasted a year and could last no more. His parents realised it was time for another move, this time far away to boarding school. Move him further outside. This time, the plan worked, as everyone there was displaced and no single group could claim territorial rights over another.

All outsiders, in a holding pattern, biding their time.

One day, shortly after leaving school and back home, he went swimming in the Forty Foot, as he often did. He was starting to change when Jack arrived. Jack was an older man, another regular who was often there at the same time as Julian.

As was his custom, Jack carefully removed each item of clothing, folded it and put it on the neat pile that he built every evening in the exact same place.

When Jack was standing naked to the world, his last act of disrobement was to take off his wig and hang it on a hook, before heading down to 'the scrotum tightening sea' as Joyce described this water by the Martello Tower.

On emerging from the sea, having first dried his head, Jack would immediately replace the wig. That done, he would stand without a stitch of clothing on, as he took his time carefully drying and re-drying every nook and cranny at ease in the knowledge that, with his wig in place, he had nothing to hide.

On this evening, he turned to Julian and said, 'Are you married?'

'No.'

'Ah ha!' mused Jack. 'Well, if you were, would you let your children see you naked?'

'Of course,' Julian replied.

'Ah ha, I see, but would you let them see their mother naked?'

It was as if he had sprung the unanswerable question and his eyes glistened with anticipation of Julian's answer.

'Of course,' said Julian.

Jack was shocked, he visibly moved back a pace as if their proximity was suddenly dangerous.

'But would you not be afraid that they would tell their friends that they had seen their parents naked?'

'So what?' said Julian.

'So what?' said Jack. 'So what indeed?'

'Would you not be afraid that everyone would think you were Protestants?'

Ireland in the 1980s.

Just when he thought it was safe to stop looking over his shoulder, he realised it was still staring him in the face.

But Julian knew already where there was a refuge. He had found it earlier on when he was fourteen and had just done his Inter Cert. He found summer work with a theatre company and it was here, for the first time, that he felt the door opening and the way forward becoming clear.

Theatre, he was to discover, is the great leveller, the great respecter of people, of dreams, of talent. Theatre is the great mother who wraps her arms around all her children and offers equal succour to all. At fourteen, he was accepted by grown men and women who had been in the business all their lives. He knew there and then that he would never leave.

He had done nothing remarkable, he had ambled though his life trying not to be different, but somehow always ending up being that way, but now he had found a refuge, a place full of people who saw no one around them as being different.

The theatre is a bizarre palace of contradictions. It is a business where an actor can have just a few bob in his pocket and still go on stage each night in a dinner jacket and be an aristocrat for two hours; it is a business where someone can grow up as a Traveller and become a national soap star on TV; it is a business where a man who spent large portions of his life in jail can be accepted and encouraged as a major writing talent. In such a profession, how could anyone be an outsider?

Theatre holds a mirror up to life. Writers create people and actors pretend to be them. Nothing is real, but everything is reality. People are cherished, nourished and important. Outsiders are welcome; in fact being an outsider is almost essential. It was here, amongst strangers, that my husband, Julian, finally felt at home, safe and no longer looking over his shoulder.

Sometimes acting can seem unimportant, trivial, even unnecessary, but it is none of those things. It is a daily reminder to us all that everyone has a part to play. Everyone, no matter how different, or just seemingly different, has something to offer, something to say and they should be listened to.

> If a man does not keep pace with his companions, perhaps it is because he hears a different drummer. Let him step to the music which he hears, however measured or far away.
> Henry David Thoreau, *Walden*

Anita Reeves

KITTY'S FOLLY

MARGARET ROCHE

Catherine McAuley's journey as an outsider began with the death of her beloved father when she was seven years of age. The year was 1783 and his death marked the beginning of financial instability for the family. She emerged out of a distinct socio-economic background where women's voices were barely heard because of massive social, cultural and political constraints. Legally women had no entitlement to vote and, once married, had limited property entitlements and were considered the chattels of their husbands. This was a brutal society where many people lived in appalling poverty, especially women.

With her mother Elinor, sister Mary and brother James, Catherine eventually moved from their family home, Stormanstown House outside Dublin, to the home of Elinor's brother, Dr Owen Conway. Some years later, when Elinor died, the three children moved into the home of a Protestant relative, William Armstrong. In this environment, there was little tolerance for the Catholic religion. Mary and James gave up the practice of their faith and, despite feeling isolated from their religious beliefs, Catherine held staunchly to hers.

In 1803, she was invited to take up residence with Catherine and William Callaghan at their estate Coolock House, as companion to Mrs Callaghan. (Mrs Callaghan was a Quaker and traditionally Quaker women have a history of philanthropy.) Quaker and Protestant women could form themselves into autonomous welfare associations within their respective churches. There was no model within the Catholic Church for laywomen to take such bold initiatives. Catholics as a class did not have the resources to initiate specifically Catholic rescue charities.

In the early nineteenth century, much of the wealth
of the country was concentrated in Dublin. Social structures were strictly hierarchical from the nobility at the
top, through the wealthy elite of merchants and distill-
ers to the poor who resided at the bottom. Poverty was
viewed as an affliction curable by the discipline of hard
work. The established Anglican Church enjoyed a special position, politically and economically, in the country. The depressed state of Irish agriculture, which lasted
from 1815 until the mid 1830s, caused many landlords
to re-examine the management of their estates. It was
no longer profitable to subdivide holdings and, with the
collapse of home spinning and weaving, evicted pau-
pers crowded from rural Ireland into Dublin city.

Severe unemployment existed among young women
in the Coolock area and, initially, Catherine acted on her
employer's behalf in dispensing charity but, aware of
the needs she found, she organised sewing co-operatives
and a retail outlet for the sale of their goods to encourage
self-reliance among the girls and women.

On William Callaghan's death in 1822, Catherine inherited Coolock House and most of the Callaghan estate, her portion amounting to about £25,000 (well over
₵1 million today). By this time, she was forty-four years
of age and, according to the annals called 'Derry Large
Manuscript by One of the First Sisters of Mercy':

> ...she lived in what is usually called good style,
> that is, she kept a carriage, dressed well, went into
> society and sometimes gave parties in her own
> house: but employed the greater part of her time
> in works of piety and charity, especially in the in-
> struction of poor children in the female schools
> of St Mary's Parish, Abbey Street.

Until the passing of the Irish Poor Relief Act of 1838,
provision for charity children in Ireland remained in-

adequate and unorganised. Catherine McAuley knew she could make a difference. She set about creating a *new way* whereby women, motivated by Christian faith, could respond to the needs of those women who lived on the margins of society.

Her inherent response towards poor and marginalised girls and women of nineteenth-century Dublin was practical and original. In 1824, she used her sizeable inheritance to purchase a site for a house on Baggot Street to provide a school for poor girls and a shelter and training centre for homeless and servant girls and women. For her, the issues were clear. Education was the key. She travelled to France in search of academic expertise and, on her return, visited the Kildare Place Society Schools. Her brother, Dr James McAuley, disparagingly called the house 'Kitty's Folly'. The premises were planned to contain apartments for ladies who might choose, for any definite or indefinite time, to devote themselves to the service of the poor without the restriction of vows.

Commitment to her dying sister's five children prevented Catherine from taking up residence when the house was opened 24th September 1827. When her brother-in-law died suddenly one year later, she became the guardian of his children too. At this time, she was the adoptive mother of at least four other children, two young cousins and two orphans. She responded spontaneously when needs arose. When a child was left homeless on the death of its mother, the care of orphans was added to the work of the institute. What is clear is that her plan was for a society of 'pious secular ladies, who would devote themselves to their service, with liberty to return to their worldly life when they no longer felt inclined to discharge such duties' (Mary C Sullivan, *Catherine McAuley and the Traditon of Mercy*).

Catherine had known the Archbishop of Dublin,

Daniel Murray, for many years as she had consulted him about religious instruction. He granted diocesan approval to the house in 1828 and gave permission to the community for the visitation of the sick, which they commenced immediately. It was not permitted at that time for the members of any religious body in Dublin to visit the public hospitals. The physicians at Sir Patrick Dunn's Hospital, knowing Miss McAuley's family and friends to be all Protestants and probably supposing she and her companions were of that persuasion, not only allowed them to speak to the patients, but also gave a general order for their admission in future. Catherine and her associates visited Mercer's Hospital, the Coombe Lying-In Hospital and the Hospital for Incurable in Donnybrook. They walked considerable distances to these hospitals from Baggot Street and in time were known as 'the walking nuns'.

Catherine had societal connections that she was not afraid to use and enlisted their aid in organising bazaars, which were patronised chiefly by Protestant friends. The women who came daily to assist in the poor school were generally educated women of independent means.

Catherine gradually formed at the house, a resident community of women who, like herself, wished to live simply and to engage in works of mercy, such as visiting and caring for the sick and dying poor. One of her stated core principles was that 'the poor need help today, not next week', and this inspired her work.

A year after the House of Mercy was opened, at Christmas 1828, Protestant and Catholic benefactors sent in contributions of food and Daniel O'Connell 'ever a benefactor to our institution' attracted great attention for the house by his attendance at Christmas dinner.

While there were many who supported her, there were others who made no secret of their disapproval. Archbishop Murray recommended that the chapel in the house be opened to the public and that the money from Sunday collections be used to support the women and girls sheltered there. This cannot have found favour with the local clergy who would not have approved of parish funds diverted in any way. The dress they adopted also 'excited the disapprobation of some who considered it an assimilation to a religious dress to which they had no claim'.

Matthias Kelly, the administrator of the parish in which the institute was situated, was prejudiced against her 'whom he considered a parvenue' and his opposition to the institute was implacable. He came to the house and said, without authorisation, that the archbishop intended giving the House of Mercy to the Sisters of Charity. This illustrates the inferior position of even middle or upper-class women in the early-nineteenth century. A member of the clergy felt free to walk into a woman's own house and tell her what was planned for its future. She wrote to Archbishop Murray and he responded by coming immediately to assure her that he never intended depriving her of her property. Because of her vulnerability, as a laywoman, she was encouraged even by friends and supporters such as Michael Blake, who was Vicar General, to move in the direction of religious life.

In order to ensure the continuance of the institute, she and her eleven associates decided to found a religious congregation of women. In September 1830, Catherine McAuley, now aged fifty-two, and two associates, entered the Presentation Convent on George's Hill in Dublin to begin an approved novitiate. The second year of her novitiate in the enclosed cloister was made very difficult by a superior who had 'opposed the admission of subjects not to be professed for their own order'. It must have been an endurance test for an independent woman of her years, yet she persevered. On 12th December 1831, the three professed their religious vows in the presence of the archbishop and left George's Hill immediately to return to Baggot Street. The following day, the archbishop appointed Catherine McAuley superior and the Sisters of Mercy was founded.

The most important of Catherine McAuley's writings is the original Rule and Constitutions of the Sisters of Mercy. The manuscript, handwritten in black ink in a copybook, is preserved in the archives of the Sisters of Mercy in Dublin. She wrote to several convents requesting a copy of their 'Rule' and the Rule from the Presentation Order (the Presentation Rule) emerged as a possibility. However, it was an issue for her that the Presentation Rule was written by a man, and therefore reflected a male perspective. So while basing her Rule on that of the Presentation Order, the Rule of the Sisters of Mercy was rewritten to reflect a woman's standpoint.

Her language about women is deliberately non-sexist. This is evidenced by her elimination of some of the more traditional patriarchal provision for female religious mentioned in the Presentation Rule. The entire deletion of the following manifests her integrity:

> When spoken to by men of any state or profession they shall observe and maintain the most guarded reserve, never fix their eyes on them, nor show themselves in conversation or otherwise, in the least degree familiar with them, how devout or religious soever they may appear to be.

As a mature autonomous woman, she would not insert a Rule for others to follow which would not apply to her. In her capacity as superior of the institute, she communicated with many men on a business level. She inspired lifelong fidelity and friendship from good men friends, notably Michael Blake and Redmond O'Hanlon.

In Part 11 of the Rule of the Mistress of Novices,

Catherine made several significant changes. She changed 'exercise them' to 'instruct them' and, in the 3rd Rule – 'She shall instruct them in modesty, meekness and humility, encouraging them to conquer those pettish and childish humours, especially in the female sex' – she omits 'especially in the female sex' a clear acknowledgment of the existence of childish humours in men too.

She had to submit her Rule to Rome and cope with alterations, which would make spontaneous admission to distressed girls and women impossible. The vast majority of Irish domestic servants were daughters of small farmers or unskilled workers. Before a girl could hope to obtain a situation, a good character reference was mandatory. By providing accommodation and references for these vulnerable girls, the House of Mercy was providing a valuable social service.

From the outset, her vision was that poor girls and women, paralysed by poverty, could be released by empowering themselves through education, in an era when girls, especially poor girls, had few opportunities to do so. Her actions give us a valuable insight into her sense of her own power and her knowledge that she could effect change.

Her compassionate sheltering of servant girls was an implicit criticism of the prevailing social system and of sexist householders within it. It is interesting to note there is not a single reference to what she was sheltering distressed women from.

Education was a maximum priority for Catherine McAuley and she made application for affiliation with the new education board in 1834. There was some hierarchical opposition to the National Schools on the basis that they would contaminate the faith of the pupils, but she saw that the new system of a planned course of study taught uniformly throughout the country, would raise the general school standard, and (ever practical) the annual grant allotted to the National Schools was very acceptable.

When Michael Blake was made bishop of Dromore in 1832, he was succeeded as Vicar General by Dean Meyler, a man who did not share Blake's regard for Catherine. One of the first things Meyler did was to contravene permission accorded by the archbishop and forbid the celebration, for the public, of a second Mass on Sundays in the chapel in the house. This deprivation caused economic hardship for the charity. Catherine's claim that the community, and fifty or sixty homeless women and young girls who sheltered in the house, had a right to a chaplain was ignored. This dispute contin- ued for some years and was the cause of great distress as her letters testify. When she informed Meyler of her intention to inform Archbishop Murray that the chapel which he blessed 'is now under some kind of condem- nation: that even a friendly priest is not permitted to celebrate Mass', his reply began thus:

> When is your procession to take place? I should like to see the Theatrical Exhibition: the Bishop must be apprised. Perhaps you may not admire the reception you will meet, for he is too straight- forward a person to be caught by your juggle.

Meyler's letters are an extraordinary expression of dis- regard for Catherine McAuley and her associates. The tone is sarcastic and bullying and one feels had the im- plication contained in the last sentence of this particu- lar letter been made to a man, it could be seen as an imputation of honour which could be challenged.

During the cholera epidemic in 1832, the Sisters of Mercy were asked to nurse the cholera victims in the Townsend Street Depot, which was converted into a hospital. At the height of the epidemic, over 600 peo- ple died in Dublin each day. Even though there were only eleven in the community, and the school for poor girls and shelter for homeless women were in full operation, four sisters served in four-hour shifts. In the period 1830 to 1841, twenty Sisters of Mercy died, five through contracting typhoid fever during visitation of the sick poor.

Every day, the House of Mercy received 'sorrowful application from interesting young creatures, confectioners and dressmakers, who at this season cannot get employment and are quite unprotected'. Many could not be admitted because of overcrowding. A legacy of £1,000 bequeathed to the institute was used to build a laundry in an effort to make the house self-supporting, since the closing of the chapel had greatly curtailed resources.

Despite the financial constraints operating in Baggot Street, the first Mercy Foundation outside Dublin was made in 1836 in Tullamore. From 1835 to 1841, Catherine McAuley founded eleven autonomous convents.

The model of leadership that she espoused is particularly striking and her approach to authority was extraordinary. She established autonomous entities, rather than keeping centralised control over the foundations. This means, of course, that she expected the sisters in each convent to respond to the local needs and concerns that they found, in a creative and responsible way. Local superiors were not encouraged to refer every decision back to her at a centralised location. This was a real breakthrough when one realises that the Catholic Church in the nineteenth century, both at a local and a global level, was promoting a centralised agenda.

The organisational structures that Catherine McAuley put in place were effective. The institution grew and thrived as the nineteenth century unfolded. An examination of the register of Mercy Sisters in the archives in Baggot Street reveals the assurance and faith

Catherine McAuley placed in her young colleagues. The women appointed as superiors to a number of these foundations were women in their twenties. A more authoritarian person than Catherine would have considered that these young women should be still subject to her authority in Baggot Street. One of her notable characteristics was the great personal interest she maintained in all her foundations and the close community spirit she fostered.

She wrote consistently what she called her Foundation Circulars to keep her communities up to date with one another. These contained House of Mercy news, social comment on events of the day and advice delivered with affection and humour. The trials of clerical interference are indulged: 'You know he has strange humours and must be honoured.' She addressed the sisters with such warmth as 'my very dearest' or 'my dearest'. Her letters define the woman she was. There are no hierarchical boundaries displayed between her and her sisters. She worked in a way we call feminist because she employed the feminist values of caring, compassion and political action, especially on behalf of poor women. She organised her foundations in a way that was as participative and non-hierarchical as one could expect to find in the twenty-first century. Despite the fact that they operated within the constraints of an ecclesiastical world, much was achieved.

The story of Catherine McAuley fascinates me. I had many opportunities in the Ireland of the 1970s to experience at first hand the position of a woman on the margins of Irish society. What a radical, upper-class, ascendancy woman was prepared to forego in order to achieve her goals continues to inspire me. The reality of life in nineteenth-century Dublin and the opposition she encountered did not deter her as she seized the opportunity to reach out to and respond to the plight of the poor. Only when it became clear that it would be very difficult for her to carry on this work outside the umbrella of religious life did she yield to the pressure to form a specific religious community. It took bravery and resilience to operate within the structures to ensure the continuance of her foundation.

It is not really possible to write today about what happened then without being influenced by what we now know; we see through a glass darkly as it were. To come to know the woman involves locating her in the context of her time, interpreting her actions and examining them in the light of the present.

In any time, Catherine McAuley emerges as a remarkable woman. She was strong and autonomous, forced to work within the system in order to have her institute survive and yet she persevered and responded to the needs of the poor in her own way. She and her 'walking nuns' refused to accept the contemporary model of female enclosed life and moved out beyond the cloister walls into the contemporary world.

Many of the challenges that women face today are similar to those that she encountered in the 1830s. The Mercy Sisters response to social needs is expressed in contemporary ways: at a global level through peace and justice issues and world debt and, on a national level, through the care of the aged, Travellers' rights and women working in prostitution. Many of the sisters now live in communities outside convent structures.

In attempting to establish a lifestyle, which is empowering both for themselves and for other women, they are preserving the imagination and creativity of Catherine McAuley and giving it modern-day expression.

Margaret Roche

THE MAN IN THE WESTERN CAFÉ

BRENDAN RYAN

Cork Simon Committee meetings twenty years ago were, to put it mildly, informal. There was no great property to manage, full-time staff were virtually non-existent and reporting and record keeping were earnest but hardly structured. Since I was chair for a good deal of that period, the level of disorder could well and justifiably be attributed to me as much as, if not more, than to Simon!

Nevertheless, real people and the shortage of money were the two main topics of all the reporting.

People who were trouble or in trouble, people who were drinking or trying to stop, people who were disruptive or co-operative, dry or wet, in or out, etc. Sometimes our categorisations were more judgemental, even if that was the last thing we intended. We had a reforming zeal that sometimes resembled US revivalism. How we reconciled that with the famed non-judgemental acceptance, I was never sure. Under a cloak of acceptance, we were, in fact, endeavouring to reform or to encourage people. Exception was often taken to people who were 'using us' though I was never sure what else people were supposed to do. Much as we would have wished otherwise, we made judgements and we fitted people into categories.

One man, however, invited no judgements and fitted no categories. How could you categorise a man who lived nowhere but didn't apparently drink, clearly didn't take drugs, kept himself remarkably clean and tidy and yet, as far as we could see, spoke to no one? He turned up in a fairly basic all-night café that our soup run used to visit at the end of a night's work. It was on the Western Road, and so was called, not surprisingly, The Western Café. He sat in a corner and spoke to no one. He was never agitated or animated, he just sat there all night. Simon people tried to talk to him, but nothing was forthcoming. Indeed, at the beginning, many wondered could he speak at all. Nevertheless, for weeks and months he featured at committee meetings. 'The Man in The Western Café' was reported on every week. Nothing changed for a long time in the reports. Week after week, people tried to talk to him. Week after week, it was reported he said nothing. He was a constant and unchanging part of our night-time landscape.

None of us, whatever our life story, are fully immune to the interest of other people. It is not our nature to live and be alone and so, gradually, conversation was entered into, though few stories of past life ever emerged. What did emerge was the fact that he was quite literally homeless. Homeless and nothing else. He was able to talk and, it emerged later, well able to read and write. He didn't drink, had no physical or mental disability and to us never showed signs of anything that could be called an illness. But notwithstanding all that, he was alone. In circumstances none of the rest of us were ever able to explain and he was never ready to talk about, Pat had lost contact with the rest of the world. He had stopped talking to it, he had no place in it, he was literally an outsider. But in his own separate outside world, he kept his dignity, his appearance and his sanity intact, apparently for years and apparently with only the rarest of contact or communication with the rest of us.

However he happened to be alone, it became apparent that he didn't simply and freely choose to be alone. His looks and his bearing made that clear. Some thing or things had happened. His face was lined, or perhaps

more aptly etched in a fashion that suggested considerable previous suffering. His bearing suggested a burden
either carried for years or still weighing him down. He
was not immune to whatever had caused his isolation.
He may have chosen isolation as the lesser of two evils,
though we will never know what the other choice was.
But the fact that he responded to gentle conversation
and was won over to trust some people, and then quite
a number of people, ought to give pause to those who
talk about voluntary homelessness and all the rest of
that sort of rubbish. Pat became isolated, became an
outsider, not by choice but by experience or perhaps
necessity. Human warmth and gentle affection changed
all that.

Pat moved out of isolation and back into a human
circle. In that circle, he not only talked but showed an
unspoiled sense of humour and a remarkable warm smile
on that heavily lined face. He made friends, in particular
with a man who was suffering from a severe physical
disability but whose sense of humour and capacity for
divilment (both inside and outside the law) was also irrepressible. Indeed, his friend always claimed that his
major source of income was work as a bouncer in a
nightclub. They became a remarkable pair. The one with
a heavily lined face, the other with limbs that were often
only marginally under his control. But firm friends they
were.

It is a remarkable story and for the rest of us con-
tains remarkable lessons. One that is obvious is about
assumptions. We assume that homelessness is caused
by more than isolation, that people cannot just drift out
and away from 'normal' living. We assume that Pat's sort
of intense isolation is a consequence of either illness or
eccentricity. We assume it can't just happen to people.
We assume that everyone who tries will succeed and we
assume that we know what success is.

Pat's is also a story about the suffering that others may go through and that we can't imagine. What's more, though, it is about the human response to intense suffering, in Pat's case literally unimaginable suffering, because none of us were ever able even to imagine what had pushed him out into such a margin of the world, caused the lines and the bowed shoulders and buried, but did not destroy, what was a remarkable spirit. Is that an argument for some view of the redemptive power of suffering? I doubt it. Pat suffered enormously and, perhaps, mysteriously and survived. But it would have been better if he had never suffered. Surely the remarkable, almost heroic, resilience that he showed would have been there no matter what happened. Surely, notwithstanding the comparatively happy ending, he could have had a full life that was as rich as the later years. Surely there is no romance in homelessness and isolation.

Even if there is no romance, there are still more lessons to be learned. One that I have learned, and that Pat epitomised, was the capacity to survive without bitterness. The Simon people I met over the years were no angels, though Pat was the nearest. Generally, they were resilient rogues who felt, perhaps justifiably, entitled to liberate what they could from shops and citizens alike. But they rarely hurt anyone other than themselves and their friends. And even then they were resilient and romantic, in a maudlin sort of way. Prison was a nuisance that was never welcomed but which was tolerated with reasonable good humour and laughed at in hindsight.

The big occasions of the year remained just that. Anyone who has ever attended Christmas in a residence for the homeless will testify to their faith. Anyone who has sat down to talk with them will come away astonished by the lack of bitterness about life that is shown. Indeed, I have found more bitterness about the comparatively minor deprivations of the affluent middle classes than ever I met amongst the profoundly victimised of whom Pat was the perfect example.

And, of course, there is another lesson. Every human being is worth talking to. Every human being, however cut off, will be the better for the efforts of others to make contact and to make friends. That is not to say that every encounter will end in the way Pat's life changed, but it is a safe bet that while we may not see the consequences, human contact is always good for humans whom life has squeezed towards the margins. It is surely better to tell a human being to f**k off than to sit in total isolation and talk to no one ever! Not that such a word ever crossed Pat's lips.

Pat moved into a council flat, where he lived near his new buddy. He never exactly became an entirely social animal, but grew to like and trust those from Simon whom he knew. But he had stability, friendship, human contact and a good deal of fun. For years, he sent me a religious calendar at Christmas with a few words of good wishes for myself and my family. If we met in the street we would talk about his flat, about religion (he was, unlike his buddy, very religious) or the weather. He had obsessions and he had suspicions but he came back from a place the rest of us have never visited and the emotional price he paid on his journey we never really knew. Probably, he was always a little bit of an outsider. But his life touched others and, it seems to me, rewarded others. His life, like many of our outsiders, probably enriched us more than all our ministrations enriched his. Like many of life's real victims, he left the rest of us with little or no excuse for our moaning about the minor discomforts that we consider suffering.

Brendan Ryan

LAFCADIO WHO? RATHMINES BOY MAKES GOOD IN JAPAN

PADDY SAMMON

Many of us take for granted some elements that make us what we are, as well as part of a group: our names, our parents, what we look like, memories of growing up perhaps with brothers and sisters, the language we speak, the place we call home, our neighbours, friends, household pets, our homeland. If many of these elements are missing, we can talk of being outsiders: people who are excluded, or exclude themselves, from the group. Outsiders can be 'dark horses' coming from nowhere and succeeding: Patrick Lafcadio Hearn (1850–1904) was all of these.

The distinctively named Lafcadio Hearn, as he is best known, died in Tokyo almost one hundred years ago, in September 1904. He was an author, translator and educator. While not well known in his ancestral Ireland, where he lived as a boy, he is highly regarded by the Japanese as the first Westerner to truly understand their culture and interpret it to the West. Although he always wrote in English, his Japanese wife, Setsu, helped him gain great insight into traditional Japanese customs and folklore at a time when, in Japan, interest in these things was dying out. Nowadays, those Japanese people who want to learn about the long-lost atmosphere of 'Old Japan', turn to the many books written by Hearn. Japanese schoolchildren learning English at school often read from his works, especially his shorter stories.

He had a great interest in the natural world, particularly insects. His powers of observation were heightened compared to the rest of us and much of his writing focused on ghosts and the ghoulish.

His father's people had been Dubliners of Anglo-Irish stock for several generations, many of them army surgeons. How his father came to be on the Ionian island of Santa Maura (or Lefkas), which lies south of Corfu, is less strange than it might seem. Since 1864, Lefkádha, as it is now known, has been a part of Greece: it's the island off which the Onassis family has their private island of Skorpiós. The Ionian Islands were long held by the Venetians, then came under French and ultimately – with the defeat of Napoleon – British rule.

Lafcadio's father, Charles Bush Hearn, went through a marriage ceremony with a girl called Rosa Kassimati, and their son, Patrick, was born on 27th June 1850. When Charles was posted to the West Indies, Rosa and Patrick travelled to Dublin. On their arrival in August 1852 they lived for a while in 48 Lower Gardiner Street, now called The Townhouse (there's a picture of Hearn on the sign outside). Rosa did not speak English, was not accepted by Charles' family, and soon returned to Corfu, never to see her child again. The marriage was annulled (either because she had completed the register with an X, or because it was not recognised, being an Orthodox ceremony in a British territory). Charles visited his son occasionally and arranged for Patrick to stay with his grand-aunt, Sarah Brenane, before he married a wealthy widow in 1856 and, when Patrick was only seven, disappeared out of his son's life. He died not long after.

Patrick was brought up in Leinster Square, Rathmines. He lived with his great aunt for a while at 21 Leinster Square (now renumbered No. 30 and not the one with the plaque!) and then in the nearby 3 Prince Arthur Terrace. These houses have change little since they were built around 1850. In 1856, they moved to another rented house at 73 Upper Leeson Street. Sarah Brenane had converted to Catholicism on marriage and her ways were strict. Parick was unhappy, and took comfort in reading. He was educated at home, before going to boarding school in England.

Patrick did not write much about his childhood, and we can only speculate on influences from his Dublin boyhood. For example, some of his keen interest in insects may have been helped by proximity to the recently opened Natural History Museum in Merrion Square.

When Sarah Brenane was defrauded of her wealth by a relative, Patrick was taken out of school and left penniless. At this stage, he abandoned his first name and called himself Lafcadio (itself surely a mistake for Lefcadio – the Greek island is Lefkas or Lefkádha). He took off for the United States at the age of nineteen, where he made a living for himself as a crime reporter with the *Cincinnati Enquirer.*

In summary, by the time he was a teenager, Patrick had left the land of his birth; been abandoned by his father and mother, whose marriage was annulled leaving him illegitimate; practised a religion that the rest of his family did not approve of; and, to cap it all, lost the sight of his left eye in a scrap at school when he was sixteen. No doubt he was also conscious of his darkish skin and small stature.

At twenty-seven, he moved to New Orleans, ending up as editor of the *Times-Democrat* and, ten years later, to the French West Indies, to St Pierre on the island of Martinique. He published books on Creole proverbs and Creole cuisine (Hearn is the first writer in English recorded as using the word Creole referring to language).

He worked as a reporter in New Orleans where he wrote his first novel *Chita.* It was in New Orleans, when covering the World Industrial Exposition of 1885, that he first became fascinated by Japanese culture as he studied the Japanese exhibit.

Lafcadio Hearn virtually invented the perception of New Orleans as a kind of alternative reality to the rest of the United States, e.g. in *The Glamour of New Orleans*:

> There are few who can visit her for the first time without delight; and few who can ever leave her without regret; and none who can forget her strange charm when they have once felt its influence. And assuredly those who wander from her may never cease to behold her in their dreams – quaint, beautiful, and sunny as of old – and to feel at long intervals the return of the first charm – the first delicious fascination of the fairest city of the South.

During the Exposition of 1885, Lafcadio became friendly with the commissioner of the Japanese pavilion and, in 1890, took off for Japan on an assignment for the Harper Publishing Company. He arrived in Yokohama, the port for Tokyo, in April 1890 aged forty, and thereafter never left the country. Japan had been opened up to the rest of the world in 1854, and the Emperor Meiji, who moved the capital from Kyoto to Tokyo, was interested in all things Western. The country was in the process of throwing out much of its past – traditional clothing, hairstyles, swords – but this also meant that the customs and the way of life of old Japan were also being rapidly abandoned.

Lafcadio became a friend of Basil Hall Chamberlain, Professor of Japanese at the prestigious Imperial University in Tokyo, who was of the same age as him. Within a few months, with Chamberlain's assistance, Lafcadio moved to the city of Matsue, in the western part of the main island of Honshu, and taught English at two of the prefectural schools, where he was paid an expatriate's salary. It is likely that he was one of only a small band of non-Japanese in Japan outside of the large cities.

In Matsue, he met and quickly married Koizumi Setsu, the daughter of a local samurai family. What is hard to understand is that Lafcadio spoke little or no Japanese, and his wife had little English – how they communicated is not at all clear. He stayed in Matsue for fifteen months, where the cold climate did not suit his health, before moving on to another teaching position in the rather warmer Kumamoto, on the southern island of Kyushu, where he spent the next three years and completed his book *Glimpses of Unfamiliar Japan* (1894).

In October 1894, he managed to get a job as a journalist with the English-language *Kobe Chronicle*; Kobe had become an open port in 1858 and had a fairly cosmopolitan atmosphere. In 1896, he took out Japanese citizenship, and changed his name: he took his wife's surname and was henceforth known in Japan as Koizumi Yakumo. That same year, with help from Chamberlain, he began teaching English literature as a professor at Tokyo University, a post he held until 1903.

On 26th September 1904, he died of heart failure at the age of fifty-four in Tokyo. He was the first Westerner to be cremated and buried as a Buddhist in Japan. His appreciation for things Japanese was awakened from the time of his arrival there. In 1890, he wrote:

> I believe that their art is as far in advance of our art as old Greek art was superior to that of the earliest European art-groupings. We are barbarians! I do not merely think these things: I am as sure of them as of death. I only wish I could be reincarnated in some little Japanese baby, so that I could see and feel the world as beautifully as a Japanese brain does.

Even a century after his death, Lafcadio Hearn remains very much an outsider: not quite recognised in Greece as a Greek (he knew no Greek); not quite recognised in

Ireland as Irish; sometimes referred to as an American, although he was never a citizen; in fact, many Japanese assume that he was Japanese, because of his adopted name. In fact, he has some claims to be one of the first truly 'globalised' people in the world.

Paddy Sammon

INSIDERS AND OUTSIDERS IN OUR CHURCH

BISHOP WILLIE WALSH

Mary and John came to see me recently. I had met John some time ago on another issue and he got in touch with me saying that he and his partner Mary would like to talk to me.

John and his three younger brothers were taken from home when he was nine years old and placed in an orphanage. He spent seven years there. His memories are ones of total lack of love and of real brutality in the form of regular severe physical abuse. Later in life, he became an alcoholic and he also spent some time in prison. He has been free of drink for several years.

John is still angry about his experience in the orphanage, which was run by religious. He has not been to church for years and has no intention of returning to an institution 'which took away my childhood'. He speaks of his fears of any physical contact with children, even today, because of his earlier experiences. John has effectively always been an outsider.

Mary on the other hand was an insider. She had a strongly religious upbringing that took church-going and prayers as normal part of life. She married a man of similar background and had what she regarded as a happy marriage. They had one child. Then, suddenly, after twelve years together, he walked out on her and their child for another woman. Mary thought she would never again trust another man.

A few years later, she met John and, gradually, that trust is being rebuilt. He is good to her and her child. He helped her nurse her dad through his prolonged illness before he died. Mary and John have been together now for thirteen years.

Because John and Mary are not married, she stopped going to church some years ago. She felt it would be hypocritical to continue going. She had become an outsider. She has recently started going to church again but she still feels like an outsider because she cannot receive Holy Communion. She is hurting a great deal because of this exclusion. She read recently that some rich person who was married for years had got an annulment – 'the rich people can always get these things but we can't'.

What am I to do as a priest? In their present situation, they cannot be married in church unless Mary gets a decree of nullity. We talk of pursuing that option – a safe option for me as an insider. But what if Mary goes down that road and at the end of three or four years her petition for nullity is turned down? Another rejection, another exclusion. Do I want to risk adding to her sense of 'outsideness'? Do I want to further add to John's understandable antipathy to that cruel, abusive institution? Or do I become the outsider who tells them not to worry about the Church's law and simply to trust that God's love and care for them is greater than any Church law? And do I become a further outsider by praying with them and asking God to bless and enrich their love and their union – a union that will always leave them outsiders?

But then Jesus always seemed to have a special care for outsiders – the lepers, the woman accused of committing adultery, Mary of Magdala, the tax collectors and sinners. Indeed, by his very association with outsiders, he became an outsider himself.

Insiders and outsiders – John and Mary will probably always be outsiders. I'm honestly not sure about myself – sometimes insider, sometimes outsider, sometimes maybe both at the same time and that I find the least comfortable place of all.

Anyhow, Mary and John, I do hope that your love

will grow and develop and ease some of the awful hurt which you have experienced.

I just think that after all your pain you deserve some real happiness in your lives.

Bishop Willie Walsh

BIOGRAPHIES OF CONTRIBUTORS

Maeve Binchy
Maeve Binchy is an international bestselling author.

Gerard Brady
Gerard Brady is a barrister living in Dublin.

Gerard Byrne
Gerard Byrne is a freelance actor who is perhaps best known for his role as Malachy in RTÉ's *Fair City*.

Mary Condren
Mary Condren is author of *The Serpent and the Goddess: Women, Religion and Power in Celtic Ireland* (New Island: Dublin, 2002), and has also written numerous articles on theology, feminism and feminist theory. She is director of the Institute for Feminism and Religion, and a Research Associate at the Centre for Gender and Women's Studies, Trinity College Dublin.

Catherine Cleary and Richard Oakley
Catherine Cleary is a senior reporter for *The Sunday Tribune* and Richard Oakley works for *The Sunday Times*.

Oliver Connolly
Oliver Connolly is a medical practitioner in Dublin's inner city.

Bernadette Cronin
Bernadette Cronin is a senior counsel, having been called to the Bar of Ireland in 1978 and taken Silk in 1997. She

regularly sits as a member of the Refugee Appeals Tribunal. She enjoys painting and had a successful first exhibition of her work in 2000.

Anne Daly
Anne Daly is an award-winning film-maker, journalist and co-founder of Esperanza Productions.

Séamus Dooley
Séamus Dooley was born in Ferbane, County Offaly in 1960. He is Irish Secretary of the National Union of Journalists. Prior to his appointment as a union official, he worked as a national and regional journalist in the *Irish Independent, Roscommon Champion* and *Tullamore Tribune*. He is a graduate of the College of Commerce, Rathmines.

Tim Doyle
Tim Doyle is a Kerry-born Garda Inspector based in Dublin and author of two books – *Peaks & Valleys* (1997) and *Get up them Steps* (2001).

Danny Erskine
Danny Erskine is a sixteen-year-old student in Ashfield College, Dublin.

Bernard Farrell
Bernard Farrell is a playwright whose work has been mainly premiered at the Abbey Theatre and also at The Gate, Red Kettle Theatre and extensively abroad.

Tony Gill
Tony Gill is a poet and one who sees himself as an outsider.

Ann Higgins
Ann Higgins is co-founder of Kileely Community Project with the women mentioned in her piece. She is co-ordinator of the Targeting Educational Disadvantage Project in Mary Immaculate College, Limerick.

Con Houlihan
Con Houlihan is a Kerry-born writer and film-maker living in Dublin. He describes himself as not yet having won the Noble Prize for Literature but was voted Kerry Rugby Player of the Year in 1967.

Tim Hyde and Geraldine McAuliffe
Geraldine McAuliffe is a nurse and Deputy Director of Trust. Tim Hyde is a Captain in the Church Army, St Patrick's Cathedral, Dublin.

Miranda Iveagh
Miranda Iveagh is a trustee of the Iveagh Trust, which was founded in 1890. She is interested in the arts, restoring old buildings and is widely known for her philanthropic works. She lives in England.

Michael Kavanagh
Michael Kavanagh is a paper vendor who has been working on Grafton Street for twenty-five years.

Eamon Keane
Eamon Keane is a freelance radio producer and singer-songwriter.

Grainne Kenny
Grainne Kenny is President of EURAD (Europe Against Drugs) and she is on the board of directors of Drug Watch International USA. She has received the

following awards in recognition of her work: Woman
of Europe Award, Medaille de Marie de Strasbourg,
Medaille de Marie de Paris, Swedish Parent Award, Lord
Mayor's Award Dublin. She lives and works in Dublin.

Gene Kerrigan

Gene Kerrigan is a Dublin journalist and the author of
Hard Cases, Another Country, How to Succeed in Irish Politics
and (with Pat Brennan) *This Great Little Nation.*

Hannie Leahy

Hannie Leahy is a founder member of the First Country Market in Ireland in Fethard, County Tipperary,
which was founded in 1947. She is currently the Market's Honorary Secretary.

Gordon Linney

Gordon Linney is Church of Ireland Archdeacon of
Dublin and a former Honorary Secretary of the General Synod of the Church of Ireland. He is married with
three grown-up children and lives in Glenageary, County
Dublin.

Ray Lynott

Ray Lynott worked for twenty-seven years as a RTÉ
Radio announcer and producer, and has also written a
collection of stories, *A Year in the Country*, which was
published by Co-Op Books in 1978.

David McConnell

David McConnell is a Professor of Genetics in Trinity
College Dublin and Chairman of the Board of The Irish
Times Trust.

Mamo McDonald

Mamo McDonald is well known in Ireland for her leadership of the Irish Country Women's Association in the 1980s. She was Chairperson of Age and Opportunity between 1988 and 2001 and is its current Honorary President. She is on the Steering Committee of the Older Women's Network. At age seventy, she went to university to study for Higher Diploma and Masters Degree in Women's Studies.

Christy Moore

Christy Moore is an internationally acclaimed singer-songwriter.

Michael Moriarty

Michael Moriarty is a judge and Chairman of the Payments to Politicans tribunal.

Vincent Murphy

Vincent Murphy lives in Fethard, County Tipperary. He runs a family pub (McCarthy's Bar which is known worldwide) and undertaking business, which has been in his family since the 1840s. He is married to Sarah who moved to Ireland from New Zealand. He has just finished writing his first book, which is a humorous account of life in the undertaking trade.

David Neligan

David Neligan was a political assistant to Dr Noël Browne from 1968 to 1982. He has a dental practice in Dublin.

John J O'Connor

John J O'Connor is a Consultant Psychiatrist in Beaumont Hospital and Clinical Director of the National Drug Treatment Centre, Trinity Court, Dublin.

Padraig O'Morain

Padraig O'Morain is a journalist living in Dublin, writing on health, social affairs and mental health issues. He was born in Ladytown, County Kildare in 1949 and has worked in journalism (staff journalist with *The Irish Times* until 2002), social services (National Social Services Board) and public relations and had a brief and undistinguished career as a civil servant at the District Veterinary Office in Naas, County Kildare. He writes poetry very early in the day and his work has been published in many literary magazines in Ireland and the UK. He is very interested in mental health and psychology, particularly in Dr William Glasser's Choice Theory and Reality Therapy. He is married with two children.

Mary O'Rourke

Mary O'Rourke is a former teacher and minister and is currently leader of Seanad Éireann.

Micheal O'Siadhail

Micheal O'Siadhail is a poet who has published many books of poetry, his latest include *Our Double Time* (Bloodaxe, 1998), *Poems 1975–1995* (Bloodaxe, 1999) and *The Gossamer Wall: Poems in Witness to the Holocaust* (Bloodaxe, 2002).

Nora Owen

Nora Owen is a former Minister for Justice.

Anita Reeves

Anita Reeves is an actor, living in Terenure with her husband Julian and two children Gemma and Danny.

Margaret Roche

Margaret Roche is former Chairwoman of AIM Family Services – a voluntary organisation dedicated to improving relationship difficulties. She is on the board of Dublin City Anna Livia Community Radio. As a mature student, she obtained an MPhil Degree in Women's Studies at Trinity College Dublin. She spent many years teaching drama and communication skills and adjudicating throughout the country. She is married with three children and likes to paint in her spare time.

Brendan Ryan

Brendan Ryan is a member of Seanad Éireann. He is Honorary President of Cork Simon Community and was its Chair from 1977 to 1980.

Paddy Sammon

Paddy Sammon lives in Rathmines and has lived in Greece and Japan. He is author of the dictionary *Greenspeak: Ireland in her own Words* (TownHouse, 2002: see www.greenspeak.info).

Bishop Willie Walsh

Willie Walsh is Bishop of Killaloe and lives in Clare.

PERMISSION ACKNOWLEDGEMENTS

The publisher has endeavoured to contact all copyright holders. If any errors have inadvertently been made, corrections will be made in future editions.

'Manic Depression' by Spike Milligan is reproduced with permission of Virgin Books.

The extract on pages 149–150 is taken from *The Broken Body* by Jean Vanier (1988) reproduced by kind permission of the publisher Darton, Longman & Todd Ltd.

The extract on page 157 is taken from *Mo Bhealach Féin* by Seosamh Mac Grianna reproduced by kind permission of An Gúm, © An Gúm, 1940.

The extract on pages 188–189 is taken from *Against the Tide* (1986) by Noël Browne reproduced by kind permission of the publisher Gill & Macmillan.

'Outsider' by Micheal O'Siadhail is taken from *Poems 1975-1995* (Bloodaxe, 1999). Reproduced with kind permission of the publisher